D1583907

In a Nutshell
Faith, Hope, Love

A Look at Love,
Relationships,
and the Power of
Believing

Eugene Christopher

ISBN 979-8-88832-093-8 (paperback)
ISBN 979-8-88832-094-5 (digital)

Christian Faith Publishing
832 Park Avenue
Meadville, PA 16335
www.christianfaithpublishing.com

Printed in the United States of America

CONTENTS

INTRODUCTION

Our virtues play a very important role in our lives. They fill us with passion and bring meaning to our very existence. So often, it seems, we take them for granted and fail to recognize their true potential. Despite our neutrality toward them, they remain constant and pure, just waiting to express themselves through our actions. It is so easy for us to get caught up in our own realities and become blind to their calling, blind to the basic truth that there is a beautiful simplicity and infinite energy that surrounds every human life... including our own.

Of all the virtues that we are capable of, there are three that stand out above them all—Faith, Hope, and Love. It can be argued that all other virtues can trace their beginnings to these three. It is for this reason that I have chosen to reflect on these virtues and our relationship to them. It is how we interact with each other in light of these virtues that ultimately define life for us. Love, especially as it pertains to relationships, is probably the easiest thing for us to relate to, but Hope and Faith are just as viable and just as critical to our existence. We need to reclaim them in our lives. It is my hope that by exploring these virtues and the importance of our relationships, we will somehow revitalize our desire to make them a part of who we are and find a home for them in our hearts.

CHAPTER 1

Will Love Find a Way?

What more to life is there?
Than to grow in its light,
Fill it with love,
And give it back…
A more perfect entity.

Many years ago, when I was in college, I took a creative writing class. One of my many assignments was to come up with a poem. I was worried about making sure the metrics were just right, and I was fulfilling all of the requirements of the assignment. I just wanted to get it done and out of the way. Still I wanted my poem to say something, so I wrote about my favorite topic, love. What came out on paper is what you see above. It seemed like a nice thought at the time, but I had no real insight into what I was trying to say. As I read this poem in my later years, I see these words with so much more clarity, and each time I read it, I get a new perspective on things and find different meanings to those words, so much so that it makes me wonder, was I really that smart? Were my best years all those years ago? Who would have thought that the twenty-one-year-old version of me could be so prophetic! I have since written many things about my favorite topic. Each time, it seems, I make a new discovery about myself and what love really means to me.

Most of us identify with love through our relationships, and understandably so. Love, more than any other virtue, focuses on "the other." After all, it is how we relate to each other that often brings meaning and worth to this life. But love is so much more than our relationships. Love is an entity unto itself, and it manifests itself in so many different ways. Our relationships are just one special way it does that. Still, this is how the vast majority of us relate to love. The vast majority of us have all pictured ourselves falling in love and getting married. Just saying that last sentence predisposes the idea that we must meet someone in order to find love. Is it any wonder we put so much pressure on ourselves to find the right one? The truth of the matter is we do not fall "in" love, we fall "with" love.

In fact, sometimes, our relationships can actually complicate the simplicity and significance of the virtue if we are not careful. It is for this reason we need to understand our relationships even before love enters into the picture. We can all agree that relationships are a commitment, and it is fair to say that marriage is the biggest commitment of them all. Love, on the other hand, is not a commitment. Love is simply a way of bringing blessing to that commitment. Both, therefore, must be cared for and nourished as unique entities. Even though they go hand in hand with one another, they need to be reconciled as two separate components. Couples in long-term, meaningful relationships are especially in tune to this message. We can learn a lot from their example.

Growing up, I was blessed with parents who were very diligent when it came to their family and their relationship. Life lessons were dealt with in a spirit of teamwork and cohesiveness that seems to be a rare commodity these days. I admired their spirit and fortitude. They were not what anyone would consider doting. We were not told how much we were loved all that often, but we were shown how much we were loved almost daily. It was the kind of love that made you feel welcomed, accepted, and part of something special. Many of these observations could not be made growing up, however. They required the kind of reflection that comes with age, and like the poem, wherein I get different insights to each time I read it, I get the same degree of varying insights each time I reflect on how I was raised. I knew nothing about what was going on when I was growing up. I didn't have the first clue as to what formula was being used to create such an environment. I'm not sure they did either.

I was seldom told how much I was loved, but I knew in my heart that I never felt more loved, so much so that I didn't even think to ask… I just knew. I learned some valuable lessons as I look back, and I am thankful for the freedom to discover those truths in my own time. As it turns out, wisdom is quite often not a question of experience so much as it is a product of reflection.

What was it that made their marriage work? Why wasn't there a recipe or template for producing the magic they created? Even now, I don't know how they did it. Maybe there isn't such a thing as a blueprint for a successful marriage…but maybe there ought to be? I remember my parents rarely fought. Sure, there were many frustrations and varying opinions, but there were no real arguments. They trusted each other enough to do the right thing. I remember they were very accepting of each other as well. It wasn't so much a case of them seeing eye to eye on things as it was recognizing that there were different ways to achieve the same goal.

Recognizing and developing each other's strengths, I think, was a key part of their chemistry. So there you have it—trust, acceptance, and support can be considered vital ingredients to a successful relationship. Sounds cliché enough, doesn't it? Of course, observing this and figuring out how they did it were two entirely different things. What was the formula that made it all work? I did not have a clue. All I knew was I wanted what they had! Maybe that is why the subject of love and relationships intrigues me so.

I always had an idea in my mind as to how a marriage should work because of their example. To this day, I have this idea in my head, and maybe it has turned me into somewhat of an idealist. Maybe it has caused me to become the hopeless romantic that I am. Is that a good thing or a bad thing? Believe me, I have spent a lot of time questioning and justifying that position. I guess I am an idealist in many respects, but I am not so sure we aren't all idealists in one way or another. Anytime we find ourselves hoping for something we are daring to dream…daring to reach for the ideal. For that reason, it is fair to say that idealism is nothing more than the heart's wish for reality. We all participate in it, just some more than others. We all picture our lives to be perfect when we are young. We always hope things will go "just right."

Of course, we by no means live in a perfect world. Idealism can be considered a pipedream, I get it. But aren't these dreams, these ideas, the thing that drives us on and motivates us to make the world a better place? Don't we all cherish ideal situations? Doesn't it make our day when we get to or from work with no traffic problems? Don't we feel great when we approach the day prepared? Or when everything we studied for on a test was covered in the exam? We have all had the experience of feeling like we were in the right place at the right time. Coincidence or not, it was an ideal situation. Idealism may be a pipedream, but it is a dream worth striving for and working toward…and that is a key point to remember. For what is more ideal than love?

As it is, reality and idealism are two completely different things, and we must deal with the problems at hand. Situations, people, ourselves…nothing is perfect. We have to navigate a sea of chaos to find normalcy, let alone perfection. Ideal situations are very nice but rare and certainly not something we can come to expect. What we can expect is quite the opposite. Our situations are not ideal and, in many instances, very hard to deal with. When this happens, many of us have a tendency to shy away and take the path of least resistance. I know, I do this a lot of times. We would prefer not to make waves and just accept things as they are. We pick and choose our battles based on our own value system, and we are more likely to stand up for ourselves in the battles we think we can win…the things we know we can change.

Change is not an easy thing for anyone, not even the person wanting the change. But when we see the purpose and good behind it, it becomes less of a hardship. We just have to allow it to happen, adjust to it, and trust it will be okay. Very often then, when we look back, we realize how good the change was, and we wonder how we ever got along without it! That, in a nutshell, is what idealism does for us! Idealism is the desire to make a change for the better. And even if these changes fail, they still raise our awareness of the problem and create an opportunity for improvement. Idealism drives that awareness. Idealism is a part of our reality, even when our reality isn't perfect! This is something else to keep in mind as we move forward.

We have all heard the story of Thomas Edison who, when asked about his many failures in his attempts to create the light bulb, very succinctly stated that they were not failures at all but rather lessons on how not to make a light bulb. Recognizing that setbacks are sometimes a part of change, we can gain better insight into what works. We are also challenged to become more resolute in our efforts to make it work. When what we are striving for is worth that much, it is worth the cost. How much is love worth to you? These same principles could and should very easily be placed into our blueprint for a successful relationship. Maybe that "striving for idealism" is the undercurrent that drives us to succeed together. Perhaps that is the key ingredient to teamwork.

Love really is a great example of idealism. It could be argued that love is idealism at its best! Just as our ideas drive us to create better things, love is the driving force that motivates us to make ourselves a better person. And just as idealism is a part of reality, even when things are not perfect, so it is with love. Love gives us the opportunity to change our hearts for the better, even when the world around us is suggesting otherwise. Let's be honest, changing our hearts can be the biggest change of all! And those of us who think we do not need to change are, more often than not, the ones that need it the most. Just like all change, learning to love creates similar awareness, it creates similar setbacks, and it creates similar opportunities for improvement. And just like change, when we see the good and the purpose behind it, it is not a hardship, and we wonder what we ever did without it!

That being said, we are not making a light bulb, we are not creating a commodity that can be sold for shares on the stock market. We are embracing something much more viable, much more personal, and much more vulnerable. I believe this is where many of us draw the line. It is very hard to risk the essence of who we are inside for only a chance to find a deeper level of happiness. Many of us would rather keep the status quo than potentially risk it all. This is especially true when we have tried and have been unaccepted in the past. Perhaps this is why, for so many of us, dwelling in idealism does not seem to be a realistic proposition and doing so only sets us up for failure.

When it comes down to it, however, we all need to feel appreciated, validated, and cherished in one capacity or another…we seek love. It truly is one of the great joys in life. How do we find it? And how do we know when we are loved in return? The vast majority of us grew up with love. We know what it feels like to love our families and be loved by them. That love exists because we allowed it to happen through mutual understanding in our experiences as we were growing up. So why is it so hard to do that with others when we get older? Especially when it comes to finding someone we can share our life with. Many of us would say this isn't the same thing. This isn't the kind of love we are talking about. Maybe it is and maybe it isn't, but in my way of thinking and to my point, love is love! The only thing that makes it different is how we choose to apply it and who we choose to share it with. It is at this moment that I think many of us fail to see the beauty of it all. Love is universal and all-encompassing! The manner in which we share it is what makes it unique. Likewise, it is the manner in which we share it that makes it most vulnerable.

Perhaps this would be a good time to identify what it is we are looking for. Why do I say that love is universal and all-encompassing? And, if so, why haven't I found it? Believe me, I have asked this same question many times. To answer that question, I believe it would be in our best interest if we went back to the basics. Perhaps if you and I were to look at this from a different angle, it might become easier to understand. Earlier, I mentioned that our relationships can sometimes complicate the virtue of love if we are not careful, and I think this is where we can get ourselves into trouble. Taking some time to differentiate between the two may help shed some light on the subject.

There is an element of simplicity in everything worthwhile. This has been shown to me over and over again through the years, and it is indisputable. It is the simplicity of life that keeps us grounded, keeps us in awe, and teaches us our greatest lessons. It is through these lessons that we seek the validation and cherishing that I mentioned earlier. We have done a good job of trying to complicate this truth over time, but we have never been able to hide it completely because this fundamental truth of simplicity is at the core of every existence. Not only that, but just as surprisingly, simplicity is the source of our greatest beauty. We only need to look outside at nature to recognize this truth. Our false perception of simplicity as being something void of content has kept us from realizing this. Simplicity is not doing without. Simplicity is taking what is and doing something with it! Simplicity is the logic of life, and when we use it, everything else makes sense. The examples of this are all around us!

The vast majority of us would have to agree that love is very worthwhile, and as we have noted, there is simplicity in everything worthwhile. It may be hard for some of us to comprehend, but love really is a simple thing! Love is probably the simplest thing of all but, for some reason, the hardest thing to grasp. Love seeks happiness in others, it finds peace in just being, and it waits patiently…on everything. It has no sense of time or commitment. And it certainly does not come with an agenda. It is like air that is all around us, just waiting to give life.

I usually turn a lot of heads with this comment: Love is not a choice. Most would disagree with me, but allow me to explain. Love is everywhere. It is all encompassing. And it flows through us as well as around us. I may be splitting hairs, but this is an important distinction to make. Because love is everywhere, the choice is not whether or not to love; it is whether or not to accept or share the love that is already offered us. The more we relate to that love, however it is presented, the easier it is to commit to that relationship and allow ourselves to find direction and purpose.

So why do I bring all of this up? The reality is so many of us seem to approach this entity of love with our own checklist of goals and expectations. We use them as a baseline for happiness and assume that once those things are found, love will find a way. We spend our lives searching for someone who shares our goals or has a similar checklist, and in the end, many of us compromise our search because, seemingly, love is so hard to find. Sometimes, we even look for other things that could possibly take the place of love…security being a big one. We are left with questions and fears, and we find ourselves doubting and wondering, will love ever find a way? Could it be that there was a lesson we failed to learn? Could it be that our expectations are getting in the way? Could it be that our desires for what we think will bring us happiness are keeping us from being truly happy? I am not saying we should not have feelings on the subject of relationships and what makes us happy, but we do need to be sure our checklists do not get in the way of that happiness.

The good news is love endures all things and love does find a way…but not through our meager attempts to make it happen. I can attest to this as well. Far too many times I have found myself trying to make more out of something than was actually there…all in the hopes that, this time, it will make a difference. I was allowing my expectations to dictate how I was going to feel about things. I wanted my ideas of happiness to be my reality. I found myself trying to make my relationships the source of my love, instead of my love the source of my relationships. How many of us have fallen into this trap? I am fairly confident I am not the only one. This is just one more reason treating the two (love and relationships) as two unique entities is so important.

When I was growing up, my mother used to can vegetables from the garden every year. During the winter months, she would use these vegetables to feed the family. Many times, we were asked to retrieve these jars for her, and we would help her open them while she was making dinner. More often than not, the lids were impossible to get off. My brothers and I would use them as a test of strength to see who was the strongest among us. We would spend a long time trying to get those lids off, to no avail. We tried every trick we knew to loosen those lids and earn bragging rights for the day. Finally and inevitably, we would deliver the jars to our mother with the assurance that the task was impossible. My mother would simply take the jar, tap around the edge of the lid with a table knife, and ask us to try it again.

Lo and behold, the lid came off as easily as it went on! Needless to say, our embarrassment was only matched by our frustration in not getting the lid off the way we wanted to. The point of the story is not that Mother knew best (even though she did), it is that love, like our attempts to open that jar, cannot be willed into existence, and no matter how hard we try, no matter how much we sacrifice, it cannot be made to happen simply on our own merit. We cannot manipulate love like we do everything else in this so-called reality. We try so hard to find love, instead of letting it find us. Love cannot be made to happen... It can only be allowed to happen.

Have you ever experienced the Chinese finger trap? This is another good example. The Chinese finger trap is a mesh sleeve, oftentimes made of paper that is woven in such a way that as you pull your finger away, it tightens up. When this happens, it is quite literally impossible to remove your finger from that sleeve. The key to exiting the finger trap is to relax, ease the tension on the sleeve, and slowly allow your fingers to exit. How many times have we experienced problems and chores that were just too difficult and seemingly insurmountable, yet when we take a break, relax, and try again, seemed to make the chore much easier? How about solutions that we thought would never come to us, appearing after thinking about something else for a while? These are all instances where allowing something to happen, very often, makes it happen. Okay, love is not a Chinese finger trap or a jar of canned vegetables. It is, however, a mindset, a way of life that allows us to look at things differently and grow from it. The point to be made is we cannot change love... Love changes us!

Obviously, just allowing something to happen does not necessarily mean that it will happen, especially when it comes to relationships. The point is, sometimes the missing pieces to our puzzle are right in front of us. We only need to rearrange those pieces (rearrange our filters) to look at things differently and find something truly meaningful. The trick is to recognize those opportunities and become open to the possibilities. Sometimes, allowing life to live us, instead of us living life, allows us to do just that. Again, I am not trying to say that we should not have feelings on the subject of relationships or what makes us happy. What I am saying is we need to know what is important to us. If we take the time to know what is truly important to us, then those opportunities will be easier to recognize. This is why I inferred that our relationships must be developed before love can enter. And if you think about it, our relationships cannot develop until we start relating to ourselves.

To seek what has true value to us, we need to get to know ourselves and perhaps rediscover who we are. Trust me, getting to know ourselves is not as easy to do as we may think. Life has a way of taking us through a maze of twists and turns. Many of us have lost that sense of who we are. But once we rediscover ourselves, we can get to the root cause of our feelings so we can know what to be open to and value. Hint: financial security, material gain, and social status are not a root cause for anything. Look deeper.

In many large businesses and schools, they have leadership skill classes. In these classes, they talk about finding root causes. They teach that the best way to get to the root cause of a problem is to ask the question "why" up to five times until you cannot answer the question anymore. I guess the five-year-olds have it right! Let's try this exercise with a couple of our so-called root causes above. Maybe it would go something like this…

- Social status is important to me when I get married.
- Why?
- Because I want to feel important and have people look up to me.
- Why?
- Because I feel like I have something to say.
- Why?
- Because no one ever listens to me now.
- Why?
- Because no one seems to care about my opinions.
- Why?
- Because no one understands me.

Gee, I just got to know you better! You are not looking for social status, you are looking for understanding. That really opens up the possibilities! I am a "nobody," but at least I can take the time to listen and understand you. I don't have to be a prominent figure in society to do that! If you take the time to look for understanding in people rather than in the society page, wouldn't that make you happier? Let's try another one…

- I want to marry for financial security.
- Why?
- I don't want to have to worry about money.
- Why?
- Because life is hard enough, I want to be taken care of.
- Why?
- Because I need to look out for myself. No one else will.
- Why?
- Because no one cares about me.
- Why?
- Because no one appreciates who I am.

Well, thank you for sharing! I feel so much closer to you now! I am barely middle class, but I can certainly appreciate you! I don't have to own a million dollars to do that! If you took the time to look for appreciation from others rather than the bottom line, wouldn't that make you happier? Wouldn't that be worth a million dollars to you?

Getting to the root cause of our feelings allows us to put things in perspective. Of course, who doesn't want to be well-liked and financially secure? We should always try our best to do what it takes to survive this reality and plan for our future. I am not trying to downplay either one. All I am saying is we should not look at them as end-all goals for ourselves but rather a means to an end. Neither notoriety nor money has guarantees. Either of them can be taken from us in a heartbeat. Knowing our true source of happiness in its simplest form, however, can never be taken away because it becomes a part of who we are.

When it comes to relationships then, when we recognize these strengths in others, we find someone we can relate to. This allows us to nurture our self-awareness as well as theirs so we can suffer these other losses and still have something to hang on to and rebuild from. In other words, when we have that foundation of happiness, everything else may come with time…and if it doesn't? Guess what? We may be less comfortable, we may be less well-known, but we are still happy! It is a classic case of want versus need. I am sure we all know someone who has a very comfortable life, but their needs are not being met and they are not happy. Likewise, we probably know people who do not have two dimes to rub together but seem to be very happy and high on life. And, of course, there are the rare few who have both (want and need). Talk about ideal situations.

Understanding what makes us happy will help us relate to reality in a different way. Things that seemed important to us before may not seem as important anymore. Basically what we are doing is getting in touch with our core values. Armed with those values, we can see with more clarity what has value to us and what just makes us feel good. The neat thing about it all is that invariably, the things that are truly important to us can give us both value and enjoyment!

- Love and idealism are a part of reality, even when things are not perfect.
- Don't let expectations get in the way. Be open.
- Find out what is important to you. Ask why.
- Nurture your self-awareness through core values. Align your filters.

CHAPTER 2

Making Ourselves Loveworthy

Let's visit our blueprint and see how it is coming along… Let's see, we need trust, acceptance, and support, check. We observed that we must have the courage to think ideally and learn to grow with every change, check. We need to get to know ourselves and allow for mutual understanding, be open to love and allow it to happen, then we must channel that love in a way that brings meaning to each other, based off of our core values. I must say, this is getting rather complicated, and we are just getting started!

All of this is good stuff! We are gaining a lot of insight into what makes us tick and what to look for in a lasting, loving relationship. The list is getting longer and may even make sense to us. It could be that this is something we already knew or have thought about before. All that being said, we are still left with the dilemma of how. How do we make this stuff come to fruition? Fine, we cannot make love happen. We need to allow it to happen…whatever that means. How? It is true that we cannot make love happen. We can support it, nourish it, and even make a home for it, but we cannot create it. Love is a breath of fresh air. It is a climate that we are blessed to be a part of and living in. What we need to do is expose our inner selves to that climate and "breathe!" We need to make ourselves loveable, or more accurately, loveworthy. Well, gee, how do we do that? What if I told you, you have known all along. Let's look at this for the simple thing that it is.

Have you ever observed young children at play? There lies the key to our answer. I know what you are thinking but bear with me. There are few things in this world as precious, innocent, and full of wonder as children. They truly make me smile from the heart! Let's look at our formula so far and see how they compare. We observed that we need to be trusting, accepting, and supporting. What child does not embrace all of these qualities? We need to learn to challenge setbacks and think ideally. What child does not think that anything is possible? And how many times, when we tell them that something is not possible, we are met with that most difficult question again: why? We learned that we need to allow love to happen and channel it toward the good of others. Have you ever watched children look out for one another and help without condition and with no regard for what it means for them? I am reminded of the book written by Robert Fulghum, *All I Really Need to Know I Learned in Kindergarten*. Wouldn't it be great if we found someone that made us feel that happy? Someone who could make our hearts leap for joy simply by being who they are? So let's find out how! What secret do those children have that we do not seem to be privy to? How do we do it?

The only answer to that question that makes sense to me is we do it through forgiveness. Children are the most forgiving creatures on earth! It is only right that they should be loved as dearly as they are. Love really is everywhere, and it longs for a forgiving spirit. Those who are truly in love cherish, forgive, and accept without anger, without expectation, and it is a mutual undertaking. I cannot stress that enough, when it comes to relationships, it must be *mutual*. Perhaps we are getting ahead of ourselves just a bit. We are still trying to make ourselves loveworthy after all. The best way I know to do that is by developing a forgiving spirit. I am reminded of a quote I had written a while ago:

Find forgiveness by forgiving.
Find hope by instilling truth.
Find faith by testifying to the truth.
Find love by doing all three.

Forgiveness is the surest and quickest way I know to make ourselves loveworthy, and it sounds like such a simple thing to do! In the previous chapter, I talked briefly about change and how a change of heart is the hardest change of all. Forgiveness opens the door for that change. If you take nothing else away from this chapter, remember this: before love can be found, we must begin by forgiving ourselves and coming to peace with who we really are. We need to seek reconciliation…with ourselves.

For far too many of us, this is a most difficult task, and for some, it seems an impossible task. For some of us, it is a moot point. And for a rare and precious lot of us, it has been a blessing. I should think the reason for forgiving ourselves is obvious. If we cannot forgive ourselves, we cannot learn to truly forgive others. We have all had exercises in forgiving. We were excellent at it when we were young children. We could forgive just about anything…including ourselves…without giving it a second thought. We can all probably think of instances when we have displayed true forgiveness. Over time, our ability to forgive became harder and harder to do. We became more critical of our surroundings and especially of ourselves as we grew into adults. Sometimes, it even seems like it is easier to forgive others than it is to forgive ourselves.

But if we cannot turn that forgiveness inward, we cannot perpetuate it in others. I know all too well how hard this can be. We have lived with ourselves 24-7 for all of our lives. We know every dirty secret of our past (and present) that keeps us from being happy with ourselves. Over time, we have beaten ourselves up pretty badly. We use phrases like "I am a loser," "I don't deserve anything," "Nobody wants to be with me," or "I am not worth anything." We measure our failures in life and transform them into some kind of a character flaw. These comments can be very humbling and keep us grounded, but I'm not sure this is the kind of ground we need to be standing on.

Unfortunately life doesn't help a whole lot. Those ideal situations are few and far between. Reality is always willing and anxious to put us in our place. I have often wondered if it was life that was putting us in our place or the people living in it that seem to be holding us down. I guess that is for another discussion. Suffice it to say that reality is sobering. It is for this reason that comparing our quest for love to young children seems to be, for lack of a better word, *childish*. We can't possibly apply that same innocence and idealism to our current reality…but that is the point. Shouldn't we try? Isn't this what we should be striving for?

My father shed some light on this for me when I was young and growing up in the '70s. The big catchphrases back then were "Do your own thing" and "If it feels good, do it." It all sounded very good but very selfish. How was I supposed to change the world in a sea of selfishness? My father was a very Catholic, Christian man. He was a proud member of the silent majority, and to be honest, he wasn't always that silent. Still he shared with me the observation that we as individuals cannot change the world per se. But if we change our part of the world for the better and have faith in others that they are doing the same, then the world DOES change. So maybe we need to focus on our corner of the world, starting with our world…ourselves.

Maybe our first step to self-forgiveness and reconciliation can be to change the things that are limiting us from relating to ourselves positively. We need to create an environment conducive to our new-found values. Reality is only real when we take ownership of what is happening and make the choice to participate in it. To change reality, therefore, change your involvement in it. Maybe we need to look at our comments in a different light. Maybe just allowing ourselves to filter things with a little more patience and positivity will help us to turn things around. I joke with my friends every year and tell them, "I am a Hallmark Christmas movie just waiting to happen!" Maybe we can put that kind of a silver lining on our self-deprecating comments. Instead of "I'm a loser," how about "I am a winner waiting to happen"?

I know that sounds a little trite, but sometimes, the smallest steps can make the biggest difference. When we take the time to put a positive spin on the things we do have to offer, it allows us to see ourselves through a filter of humility. Humility is a very endearing and important quality in people, when used appropriately. Too often, we view humility as a weakness, but it is not…it is a strength! We often equate humility with low self-esteem, but that is never the case.

Humility is simply recognizing our worth and getting the most out of it...and even celebrating it! We each have our own worth in any given situation. Do not compare yourself to others and think yourself a lesser person. You are no such thing! We all have different strengths and weaknesses. Be 100 percent of who you are. That is all that you can give, and it is all that is needed to make this world a better place.

Do what you can with what you have and just have faith that who you are is what is needed at the time. Even though it may not seem that way, there is a method to the madness. Trusting that being your true self is allowing you to be part of the solution will pay dividends in the long run because having faith in who you are allows you to have faith in other things. When you act from your core values, anything you do will be a gift to others, and you may even discover more about yourself in the process. After all, you will never find out who you are if you measure yourself by other people's actions. The best way to find yourself is to be yourself...and adjust accordingly.

As you navigate this path to self-discovery, remember to be patient and be open to the possibilities. It is hard to be patient when what you are searching for is so important, but that is exactly why patience is needed. Patience allows us to weigh our options and seek clarity. Patience is not waiting, it is contemplating. Patience is not indifference...it is knowing when to make a difference. When you are armed with the gift of self-awareness, when you know yourself and where your true happiness lies, when you develop a forgiving spirit, then recognizing those opportunities becomes easier, and you are able to act proactively to get where you want to go.

When we become proficient at self-awareness and hone the ability to forgive ourselves, we learn to start each day with a clean slate! Can you imagine the freedom this would create within us? Each day, we could rise with the understanding that "today, I am going to be the best 'me' I can be!" Of course, this is not an overnight occurrence. We may need to start small and build our way up to it, but with this foundation in place, this change becomes possible. If we ask ourselves this question: "What part of myself can I improve today?" and make that an area of focus for the day, then we are building a foundation for positive change. When we learn to make this a daily exercise, it will invariably change our filters. It will change our involvement in this reality into the reality we are looking for. But as we work on this noble endeavor, we need to remember setbacks are a part of change. We must stay the course and strengthen our resolve. Anything worth that much is worth the cost. I think we would be doing all of ourselves a big favor if we started doing that today!

For those of you who consider self-forgiveness a moot point, I beg you to reconsider. Take the time to evaluate what is important to you, and hopefully, some of the things we have talked about will make a little more sense. Ask yourself the dreaded "why" question. I think if you look deep enough, you will find it is the things that are keeping you from forgiving yourself that are telling you, you don't need to. Do not justify your existence in terms of one person. You would be missing the most important and most exciting lesson of all, if you did!

For you dear and precious people who have found a way to do it, for those of you who have that divine spark of self-awareness, for those of you who know how to start each day anew and forgive yourself with the resolve to improve, I beg you to share! It is a rare gift you have, and it needs to be shared. Maybe the things that worked for you will work for others. Maybe by being an example, your spark will rub off and shine in others. I hope and pray you will always be a light to other people. It is only then that you can measure your own worth.

I believe that forgiveness is the unsung virtue! We are discussing faith, hope, and love. But along with love, there is a fourth which is sacrifice. Sacrifice is the proof of love. I can assure you, however, there can be no sacrifice without forgiveness. Without forgiveness, sacrifice is simply a hardship. Forgiveness is the foundation on which love stands, and it is the origin of all intimacy. Before we can move forward, we must forgive ourselves and be open and resolve to improving. I may have just given you the hardest assignment you will ever have to do, but I can assure you and promise you that taking the time to become proficient at forgiveness and recognizing self-worth will open doors you never knew existed! You can move forward armed with the knowledge that you are okay! You are more than okay…you are loveworthy.

Beware! Old habits die hard. Just like every other habit, you must be diligent in your efforts to break the bad ones. You must keep your eyes on the bigger prize. The more you can do that, the easier it will get for you. Then, before you know it, you are a much better version of yourself! And who wouldn't want to see that? This is not in any way an easy undertaking! The longer you wait, the harder it becomes, but no matter how long you wait, it is so worth the effort! Remember to expect setbacks. That is part of change. Being determined to work through those setbacks, though, will get you where you need to go.

Of course, let's not forget that reality is still out there. Your checklists can reemerge at any time. Do not ignore them, qualify them based on your new resolve, and change them into something useful...even if it is only to know what not to look for. There are many opportunities for life to bring you down, so the better you become at knowing yourself, the easier it will be to "be" yourself in spite of those setbacks. As they say, there are no guarantees in life. Nothing is ever free, but as you enter into this new version of yourself, you will see that your filters have changed. You are happier with yourself, and you show it. All of a sudden, you have made yourself something others are drawn to. Others will want to know what makes you tick, and you will have a much clearer picture of what is available to you. Ask any person who has kicked a habit...any habit. I think they will agree with me. There is a revitalization that takes place, and there is a feeling of empowerment. When we experience these positive results, it strengthens our resolve. This can be yours by forgiving and reconciling with who you are and relating to yourself positively.

Being in a relationship is not for everyone. Some of us are perfectly content to share our core values with the world and not just one person. Again, that is why love is uniquely different. When we reach this level of self-awareness, our relationships can be with anything. It could be another person, it could be a career, it could be a mission, or it could be a vocation. The opportunities for expressing yourself are limitless when you know who you are! Whatever path you choose, however, find the one that brings you peace. The important thing is our lives have now become a book worth reading, and we can better accept new challenges. We have made ourselves open to the possibilities… We have created a more ideal situation for ourselves… We have made ourselves open to love. Remember, it is how we channel that love, that passion that makes all the difference. Above all, stay committed to maintaining and nurturing a forgiving spirit in whatever you undertake. Do that, and each day is a new beginning. Do that, and the challenges…as well as the rewards are just getting started.

- Get to know yourself. Be yourself and adjust accordingly.
- Humility is recognizing your worth and celebrating it.
- Patience is not indifference. It is knowing when to make a difference.
- Develop a forgiving spirit. Let the kid in you come out.
- Alter the current reality and make it your reality.
- Be a better version of yourself… Be happy!

CHAPTER 3

The Best of Everything

With the understanding that love and relationships are two unique entities, we can now approach relationships with a sense of being at peace with ourselves… We are ready to open ourselves up to others. We have our core values in place, and we now have love to share, not look for. The more comfortable we are in our own skin, the easier it will be to share with others. I have found that finding and sustaining a relationship are two sides of the same coin. They both have the same worth, but they both look different, and they need to be recognized for what they are. I often wonder how many times couples fall into the trap of not recognizing the difference. We often refer to something of great value as having "stood the test of time." While that adage is true, I would dare to qualify that statement by saying things of value have stood the test of time but also have something to show for it.

Getting to know ourselves allows us to filter things (and people) in such a way that it brings meaning and value to us. It allows us to seek understanding, which in turn helps the other person to understand. This requires patience, and it is not an easy thing to do at times. Luckily, we had experience doing this as we were growing up. We may just have forgotten. As we were discovering ourselves, we were able to form friendships and bonds that may have lasted a lifetime. We formed values and had a sense of what was really important to us. Over time, we can sometimes lose sight of that. A few hard knocks along the way, a misunderstanding, a loss of a loved one, or a broken friendship can sometimes make us more calloused toward life and cause us to shift our focus to safer things…more enjoyable things…and cause us to opt for a path of least resistance. That is why it is important to rediscover who we are, forgive ourselves, and get back to what makes us truly happy. Staying open to our values allows us to stay open to love.

The heads side of this proverbial coin seems to be the most enjoyable. For many of us, this can be considered the best side of a relationship…and what's not to love? For some of us, however, this can be the focal point for all of our relationships. Whether it is the people we hang out with or the people we call our friends, we are high on life and ready to take on the world with little regard for outcomes. As enjoyable as it may sound, however, this is when we are most prone to error, especially when it comes to lasting relationships. Friends and acquaintances can come and go. When it comes to lasting relationships, we must be more attentive. On this side of the coin, our checklists are in full throttle, and it is hard to decipher what is good and what is valued. It is on this side of the coin that we are most challenged to remain loveworthy.

Still, it is an exciting time in our life and is to be celebrated for what it is. Without it, we would be lost. The really special part of this experience is sharing our journey with others as they do the same thing (rediscover themselves). We relate to others based on our filters, and we get a feel for who we are in relation to them. Therefore when we have a true sense of what is important to us, we can identify more readily with others who feel similarly, regardless of what is popular or expected at the time. The special part is recognizing the other person's worth to us and ours to them. The people who I have considered my best friends were formed using this process.

We are all on our own journey to self-discovery. It is important to remember, though, we do not have to be "discovered" in order to form a lasting relationship with someone special. Part of the joy and bonding that couples enjoy come from discovering these things together. The important thing is to relate with each other in a way that brings us that sense of true happiness. The more we can relate to each other, the easier it is to rely on each other. Love is every-where. Deciding on how we want to channel that love and who we want to share it with makes all the difference. The more we relate to one another, the easier it is to allow love into the relationship. The easier it becomes then to decide how we want to share that love. Remember, love is part of reality, even when things are not ideal. We do not need to have all of the answers. We just need to have the right questions. When we relate, we know what questions to ask. Be patient... The clock is not ticking. But be attentive because time doesn't stand still either.

I had a conversation with a young man once. He told me that he was in love with a woman and had every intention of proposing to her in the very near future. I asked what was stopping him? He said nothing really, he just wanted to finish one last semester of school, and find a job, save some money, and get things headed in the right direction before he popped the question. I told him he was missing out on the best part. In essence, no matter how well-intentioned, he was letting his checklist get in the way! I advised him that if he truly loved this woman, to not wait. If we take the time to make sure everything is in place, we miss out on an important path to discovery with that other person.

Besides, who is to say that what you think needs to be in place is something they think needs to happen? What if his new job required him to move away? Would she like that? Should she go with him? What if her new job kept her here? Perhaps you know someone who has given a similar reason for waiting. Perhaps you have experienced that sense of making sure things were "just right" yourself before moving forward on a relationship. Isn't it interesting how we always seem to want our relationships to start out ideal?

Relating to each other allows us to experience each other in a way that gives us validation and appreciation and worth...or not. I know it sounds cliché, but we really do try each other on for size. Relating goes beyond social media, and it is important that we relate the negatives as well as the positives. Sometimes, understanding each other when we don't see eye to eye is more telling than when we do. As we take the time to get to know each other, we establish each other as best friends, passing acquaintances, or someone we can commit to for the rest of our lives. So when we have a better sense of who we are inside, we can more easily focus on getting to know others. Taking the time to do that, without jumping to conclusions, should help us find something meaningful. In many ways, that is the easy part. Recognizing that moment when we want to move forward in the spirit of love can be the trickiest part of the whole process. Certainly, it is the most critical as we commit to the relationship.

This is where mutuality comes into play. If we are not on the same page with our core values at this point in time, what makes us think we will be on the same page down the road? I think it is important, therefore, that both parties reach that same realization of what is valued, regardless of where they are in their own journey. When we have that level of mutual awareness and mutual understanding of what makes each other truly happy, then we begin to realize we have something special…something to work toward, hope for, and help each other attain. The more we can recognize that in each other (and ourselves), the easier it is to bring that to fruition. Since we are being cliché, how many times have we heard people say, "Today, I married my best friend"? Why does that make so much sense to me?

Finding our soul mate, therefore, is finding the person who allows us to love fully through mutual respect, appreciation, understanding, and acceptance in the light of that core value. The key word there being *mutual*. With mutuality, we learn to grow and rediscover ourselves as well as the other. We cherish that person as an extension of ourselves, and we cannot do anything without first thinking of the other person. Those who are truly in love exhibit this behavior, and it is effortless! Do not mistake mutuality, however, for commonality. There are two sides to every story, and there is more than one way to reach a single goal. Learning to accept each other's differences in the spirit of that single goal and growing from it allows us to understand more fully and makes it easier for us to respect and appreciate each other. I have known many couples who have failed to do this, and it has caused many problems. When we look to change the other person, we are not accepting them for who they are, we create walls between us, and forgiving becomes harder to do. When we respect each other's journey, we are better able to understand and cope… as well as help each other grow into something better. This is yet another reason mutuality is so important.

Just as the heads side of the coin is the most enjoyable, the tails side of the coin is the most rewarding. And for that reason, it requires our maximum effort. I would dare say that just as the other side of the coin is most prone to error, this side of the coin could be considered the most vulnerable, and it requires commitment. Many of us who are focused on the flip side of the coin fail to recognize this sometimes. I opened with the comment that relationships are a commitment, love is not. Love is love. It is how we choose to share it that makes the difference. We need to be able to transition from one side of the coin to the other and recognize when that change needs to happen. When we recognize that moment, we take our love and apply it to that relationship. We choose that relationship as a major venue for expressing the love we hold inside. Both sides of the coin still exist, and both can be enjoyed for their worth, but our focus needs to change to the big picture, not the here and now. We do that through commitment. Our filters need to be adjusted to include another person. Maintaining and sustaining a healthy relationship at this level requires understanding, commitment, and lots and lots of patience! The more we can relate to one another, the easier these characteristics will be to employ…but they are required nonetheless.

And let's not forget about love. Relating and commitment are not a guarantee of love. They are the backbone of a healthy relationship. Love is separate. Love is the gift we give to each other, and it must be nourished… And it must be mutual.

Of course, communication is vital to any relationship. We hear this all of the time, but it does bear repeating. We need to continually share with one another. After all, as common as our lives have become, we are still on two different paths of self-awareness. Understanding where we are on that path and helping each other grow can only be done through active sharing. It has been my observation that communication seems to be the first thing to go in a relationship. Some of that is understandable. We live with each other 24-7, and we get to know each other very well until there are no more discoveries left to be made. The everyday can become quite routine. But communication on this side of the coin is more than "Did you have a good day?" or "Did you stop at the store like I asked?" Communication also involves reflection on the other person and taking the time to appreciate and validate their feelings. It involves being in tune to their moods and reading their body language. This is easier to do when you are both relating at a level consistent with your core values.

As we move into a deeper relationship with each other, as we hone and expand our capacity for understanding and patience, we must remember to maintain our forgiving spirit. That is what got us here, and we should not lose track of that. In my opinion, the forgiving spirit is critical to sustaining a relationship. Given everything we have discussed, I believe it is safe to say that love cannot thrive without forgiveness... It will not endure without forgiveness. By maintaining a forgiving spirit, we can make sure the door for love stays open to wherever our relationships take us. A forgiving spirit supports communication because we are always seeking reconciliation, even if we have not done anything wrong.

Just taking the time to reconcile the day allows for communication and validation. When we share the day, if we talk about our reactions to the events of the day and not just the events themselves, it gives us the opportunity to understand and support each other. What a wonderful way to keep things fresh! It does not have to be done every day, but it needs to happen regularly. The more involved we become with the world around us, the more opportunities we have to share something new. The everyday becomes every day.

When we are not able to maintain a forgiving spirit, we open ourselves up to potential pitfalls. How many times have we seen relationships fall apart because one party was not able to forgive the other? Something happened, and no one is talking. One party does not want to talk about it, and the other is left wondering what they did wrong. Misunderstandings rise up, and before we know it, we are upset with each other over potentially nothing, other than lack of communication. Taking the time to reconcile the day (or week) diffuses the situation and allows for a better understanding of each other. As I mentioned before, I believe that forgiveness is the foundation on which love is built. Forgiving and reconciling are the best things we can do for one another. Remember, it is how we channel our love and how we care for it that makes all the difference...and makes it most vulnerable. Healthy, active communication is like a workout for the relationship. It makes it stronger and more emotionally fit. A forgiving spirit allows us to keep love viable and in our midst. For that reason, I believe that forgiveness is the beginning of all intimacy because it creates so many opportunities for us to share.

Intimacy is letting go of yourself and trusting that you will be okay. Intimacy, regardless at what level we experience it, requires letting go. That is why forgiveness is so important! If you think about it, in many ways, intimacy can be considered an act of forgiveness. We first need to forgive ourselves. This in itself is an exercise in letting go. As we learn to let go, we are better able to let go for others. Forgiveness needs to happen before we can reach intimacy. We must forgive...and just as importantly seek forgiveness. Both things must happen in order for love to thrive! This is another two-sided coin that many of us fail to recognize...or admit to. Seeking reconciliation as well as forgiving helps to remind us of what is important. Reconciliation implies doing better and seeking it makes it easier for others to forgive. When we forgive, we open ourselves to sharing and understanding. With understanding comes trust, and when we trust, we begin intimacy. As trust grows, so does intimacy. It is through this trust that we are able to give of ourselves, completely and honestly. Trust is the glue that holds us together. It is the ability to believe in each other and hope for the best in each other. Once we reach that level of acceptance, sacrificing comes naturally to us, for all we have learned, know, trust, and cherish about the other.

As a result of this intimacy, we also know when we have wronged the other and we need to seek forgiveness. That, my friends, is what love feeds on! The more we maintain that spirit of forgiveness and reconciliation, the more unconditional our love becomes. The more unconditional our love becomes, the easier it is to forgive, reconcile, and share in order to maintain that high level of trust. The reward for loving someone that much is exponential!

I can honestly say I have experienced glimpses of these moments of true happiness through the course of my lifetime. They are, by far, some of the happiest moments of my life! Reaching that level of awareness is one of the greatest feelings in the world! They are so profound and so complete that there are no words to describe them. They are able to fill me with so much warmth, wonder, and peace that all I can say is, "My God... Thank You!"

Have you ever loved someone that much? Have you ever had the joy of knowing someone so intimately that the mere presence of them in your life brought you that same sense of peace and wonder? This is the joy that comes from loving unconditionally. The need to be understood, to be loved are at the core of everyone's existence. When we are able to do so in a spirit of mutual understanding and reconciliation, it lifts us past ourselves and gives us a feeling of something greater...something universal and all-encompassing. The really neat thing is we are able to find it in one another.

These experiences are unlike any other! Of course, these magic moments never last as long as we would like them to. We would be foolish to think this kind of idealism could last forever. There is no way we can maintain such a high level of "mush" (no matter how much we would like to). Reality is quick to bring us to our senses, and just like the weather, we learn to appreciate the sunny days much more when there are also rainy days. That said, we are still able to visit that utopia once in a while, and that is enough to sustain us and look forward to. The more we can nurture a forgiving spirit in each other, the more visits to that Eden we are able to make. Love abides with a forgiving spirit. It is so easy when we have the best of everything to lose sight of what got us there. It is human nature. Taking the time to keep things fresh through reconciliation and active sharing allows us to stay focused and strengthen our commitment. Remember, rainbows require both sunshine and rain... Be thankful for both.

- Be open to the possibilities...and be patient.
- Seek mutuality. Relate core values.
- Love is a gift we give each other. It must be nourished. It must be mutual.

- Intimacy is letting go and trusting that you will be okay.
- Forgive and seek forgiveness… Let love thrive.
- Share often… Reconcile daily.

CHAPTER 4

When Love and Reality Collide

What a wonderful and "ideal" situation we have created! Who could go wrong with a blueprint like this? When we enter our relationships in a spirit of love, it creates an atmosphere of blessing. As we have pointed out, however, the two are not mutually exclusive to one another. When our focus turns to our reality and how we relate to it and not love (and all it stands for), we lose sight of that blessing. Life challenges us and, oftentimes, changes our perspective on what is important. Our individual paths to self-awareness can offer significant challenges to our relationships as can reality, public expectations, and our own wants and desires (our checklists). Even at our best, our core values are being tested…even attacked. Nothing about reality is ideal. Every day is a struggle to make our worlds a better place. We are continually challenged to fight through our setbacks in order to bring about change for the better. More often than not, we are forced to focus on our reality rather than our relationships… And love? That almost becomes a distant third.

I know from experience how hard and sometimes insurmountable those setbacks can be. Can you imagine how problematic those challenges would be if we did not share the same core values? And let's not confuse core values with common goals.

A common goal might be financial security, but that has nothing to do with the values you need to obtain that goal. How is your money to be made? Does it include taking advantage of others? Is that something you both can live with? How will money affect what is truly important to you? Both of you? How much money is too much? How is any excess to be shared? Will it be shared? We have all heard the saying "Money changes people," and it does. All of a sudden, our desires and wants are back on the table. Our checklists are back in all of their glory! If our core values are not shared, it can create some serious obstacles. It becomes very easy to lose sight of what is important...and lose sight of each other. How many times have we seen people drift apart because their needs are not being met? Be careful what you wish for.

A common goal might be having children, but that has nothing to do with the core values you want to instill in those children. How do you think they should be raised? What do you want them to learn from Mom and Dad? How do we manage a child with disabilities? How will we react to each other when our philosophies do not mesh? Is that okay? Children are such a gift and such a blessing, but they will expose your weaknesses quicker than anything. Likewise, they will expose strengths you never knew you had. Either way, they will challenge you and expose everything about you...both of you...and even pit you against each other. If our core values are not shared, it can create some serious obstacles in our relationships. I know of many couples who have struggled with the difference between common goals and core values. Some of them could not survive as a result of it.

Of course, children are not the culprits here. God bless them all! Children are only one of many things that can challenge the resolve of a relationship. Finances (as mentioned above), careers, lack of quality time, lack of communication, errors in judgment, and selfish acts can all play a part, and many times, they occur in multiples. I am sure you can add many more things to this list. Sometimes both parties are making mistakes, sometimes only one, sometimes neither one! How do we survive this barrage of distractions and obstacles? How do we weed through all of the perceptions, emotional walls, and ill feelings? Sometimes the problems just seem insurmountable! Many times, the answers to these questions are very hard to find. So when we do not share, when we do not reconcile with each other, these problems are only exasperated and amplified.

But when we have that common ground, when we have that shared happiness that can only come from truly knowing and loving each other, when we relate to one another in a way that keeps us centered, we are able to navigate this sea of challenges and complete our journey. Communication on a regular basis is vital to this understanding. It allows us to share our journey with each other and better understand where these challenges are coming from. Likewise, we can use these opportunities to remind each other of where our priorities lie. When we take the time to see ourselves through the other person's eyes, it allows us to better realize what direction we need to go and to grow from the experience. The benefits from this are twofold. It allows us to better ourselves, and it also validates the other person's worth to us. Simply relating to each other creates a win-win situation. When we relate, sharing is not a chore. It comes naturally.

My brother is one of my heroes. I had an opportunity to talk with him a while back. He had recently lost his wife of fifty-plus years. She died from complications with diabetes. Through the years, she had all kinds of problems, which eventually put her in a wheelchair with her legs amputated. In the last years of her life, she required a lot of medical attention, and her family cared for her 24-7. My sister-in-law was, as I would describe her, very passionate…about everything…especially her family. There were many times the perception she gave was not the most gracious, and to be honest, there were times when she simply rubbed me the wrong way. It was part of her nature, and I accepted her for who she was, but I often wondered how my brother was able to cope with it all. Obviously dealing with this disease was not the life either one of them had planned for themselves. And I know there were many opportunities for despair. While her health was failing, their son was diagnosed with cerebral palsy, and my brother had to endure his son's death within a year after his wife's passing.

It seemed that life kept giving him one blow after another, and yet his mindset was always positive, always hopeful. When I spoke with him, I tried to convey my support and my dismay over all of the things that had happened, and before I could even begin, he told me that he considered himself the luckiest man alive! For him, it had been a journey that was better than anything he could have hoped for. He considered himself blessed. Needless to say, I was humbled.

Health issues are always a hardship, and life turns on a dime. I have neither the time nor the energy to go through all of the problems, issues, and obstacles that life throws at us on a daily basis. Some of you are more acquainted with them than I. All we need to know is these obstacles are out there, and many times, our ability to forgive is severely challenged. Health and life issues are not the only thing that challenges us. Sometimes our obstacles are self-inflicted, and we jeopardize our relationship because of our own actions. Sometimes reconciliation is not possible, but with any luck, forgiveness still is. These are the situations that cause the most turmoil. When do we say we have had enough? How do we know when something is worth fighting for? How many times must we forgive? The answer to these questions can only be found within.

When we truly relate to each other, however, the answers to these questions are more easily answered. Having mutual respect and sharing regularly should circumvent many of these problems. Active sharing will help keep us focused and allow us to reconcile with one another before things get out of hand. If you think about it, it is the lack of sharing that oftentimes allows these self-inflicted wounds to take place. As I mentioned previously, the more we can maintain a spirit of forgiveness, the easier it will be to do just that (forgive). And the more we forgive, the more unconditional our love becomes. When that love is mutual, it is an amazing thing! I am beginning to see why my brother felt so blessed.

With all of the problems we endure, it only makes sense to me that it is vital for both people in a relationship to maintain that forgiving spirit. This is yet again a place where mutuality comes into play. When we do not better ourselves for the other person, we are not maintaining a forgiving spirit…we are simply taking advantage of the other person's good nature. But when we allow ourselves to love through that spirit, we learn to accept and see things for what they are. Being able to develop that gift and hone those senses together allows us to be the best version of ourselves we can be. It also helps us to recognize the best in each other and seek reconciliation when we are not at our best. We turn our negatives into positives, and we are better able to celebrate what we bring to each other. When love is experienced through a forgiving spirit, we learn…

Not to criticize but to accept.
Not to judge but to appreciate.
Not to ignore but to support.
Not to assume but to seek understanding.
Not to change but to grow.
Not to communicate but to share.

Some people are called to share their love with the world in larger venues, not just one person. However we choose to express ourselves, the concepts we have discussed can still be applied, and in some ways, simplified. We still have to relate to others, but maybe not as intimately. We still need to apply these concepts to become the best version of ourselves we can be. The need will always be there for self-forgiveness and improvement. There will always be a need for communication, commitment, understanding, and appreciation.

A different kind of casualty in the collision between love and reality are those of us who still long for and need the one-on-one relationship but have no one to share it with. How do we survive? This type of casualty can cripple our self-esteem and present us with major obstacles. How do the brokenhearted and lonely survive? I am all too familiar with this state of limbo, and it is not for the faint of heart, I can assure you. I know the pain and the ache of waiting and wondering. We feel like lost puppies in an animal shelter that no one wants to claim. It is so easy to fall into despair. We are forced to live the life of the single-hearted when all we really want and need is the opportunity to share love with someone. All we want is the chance to relate to and make someone happy. Rising above that abyss is one of the biggest challenges the lonely face. Self-forgiveness is especially hard, and self-awareness only makes us sadder.

Those of us who experience this void are all too familiar with the loneliness that comes along with it. This is when it is important for us to remember that relationships and love are two different things. Just because we have not found a life partner does not mean we are not deserving of love. In many ways, our capacity for love is much larger because of that void! We feel like our only chance for survival is to distance ourselves from the very thing we are drawn to, but in reality, we are actually embracing love even more in order to survive. We are hanging on to the one thing we know will get us through. This may not seem like a big comfort to us in the moment, but it is important to keep in mind that relationships are not the source of our love. This is where knowing our true selves will become especially important. Having faith in ourselves will allow us some semblance of peace. Still we cherish the opportunity to share with someone, and we long for that moment. In the meantime, we learn to appreciate others who are so blessed, even though our loneliness remains.

That is why there is a distinct advantage for those who are in a "real" and lasting relationship. The support those relationships give to one another on a personal level is so rewarding and so oftentimes taken for granted. There is a reason statistics show that married couples tend to live longer than single people. I believe this is it. Having that support and understanding from someone who believes in you and relies on you can add years to your life! Just talking about it makes me feel younger at heart! When we relate to one another in a way that keeps us connected, we are giving ourselves the best gift possible…life. If you find yourself in a relationship like this, please take the time to cherish. Do it now! Look past any pettiness there might be between you and smile. For the gift of understanding, which you are giving each other, is a treasure beyond measure.

When I was married, I witnessed a lot of that pettiness. It is unavoidable in any relationship. But taking the time to look past it through the eyes of understanding allows us to free ourselves from the trap of focusing on that pettiness and opening our eyes to something more important. I recall an incident where my wife had barricaded herself in a room so she could finish wrapping presents for Christmas. When the kids were little, we were so very diligent about making sure their Christmas was special. It is safe to say we went overboard every year. Not only were the gifts numerous, but I was not allowed to help with the wrapping. She insisted that she wrap each present, just so there would be no variation in wrapping, and the kids would know that they all came from the same place (the North Pole). Because the gifts were numerous, she very quickly fell behind in her efforts to get the wrapping done. The deadline for Christmas was fast approaching, and she was working feverishly to get everything done on time.

It just so happened that on this particular day, her mother had joined us for a Sunday meal, and the entire family was getting ready to sit down and eat. My wife informed us that we should eat without her, and she would grab something later…much to the disappointment of the kids and her mother. I took a moment to visit her fortress and waded through the packages and all of the strewn-out paper to talk to her quietly. I congratulated her on the great job she was doing. I asked her why she was going to such great lengths to do all of this, and she told me, "So the kids would have a good Christmas." I smiled and reminded her that her family was seated at the table, ready to eat, and waiting for her. I pointed out to her that by secluding herself, she was defeating the very purpose of why she was wrapping in the first place. I asked her to reconsider and walked away.

A few minutes later, she came to the table, and we enjoyed a very nice family dinner. Looking at the big picture sometimes allows us to look past the moment and recognize what is really important. Now that I am single, when I meet people who are caught up in that same pettiness, I just smile. I wish I could tell them it isn't worth it, but they would never listen to me.

When we truly relate to each other, pettiness is replaced by understanding as seen through patient eyes. It is this understanding the lonely long for. When we take the time to nourish our relationship and our love by not letting reality dictate how we react to each other, then we are keeping our relationships healthy and happy. When the lonely encounter healthy relationships, we are simultaneously thrilled and jealous… There is no other way to say it. We are thrilled to see how rewarding life can be, and yet we can't help but be jealous of those who experience it. We wish for it so much that we would consider ourselves the luckiest people in the world, if we had it…not unlike hitting the lottery. That is only a slight exaggeration by the way. So how do those of us waiting for a relationship survive? The answer can be varied and relative based on prior experiences, where we are in our own journeys, etc. We can become calloused toward the situation or we can embrace what is and move on. As we have seen, however, we cannot force things to happen. I can't tell you what will work best for you, any more than I can tell you how you feel.

What I can tell you is this time is an opportunity for us to hone our core values. It is an opportunity to reevaluate what is important to us and remain open to all possibilities. I know all too well how painful of a process this can be. But as with everything else, we must be open to change…and change requires forgiveness. Always remember, love longs for a forgiving spirit, so make sure yours remains intact. It is also important to make sure our checklists do not get in the way. This is very easy to do when we want something so badly. It could be that what we thought would make us happy is not the source of our true happiness. Take the time to reevaluate. Sometimes we long for something so much that we do not recognize what might be. As I mentioned before, this is a good time to embrace love as a part of reality, even when reality isn't ideal. Remaining open to love with a faith in ourselves will help us navigate this difficult time in our lives. Maybe just helping other couples recognize the blessing they have in each other will get us through. Maybe this is our calling…maybe that is what I am doing right now.

As lonely as those of us without a life partner may seem, there is one situation that I would consider worse, and that is loneliness within a marriage. This is where love and reality can truly collide. In addition to the difficult sea of feelings and emotions described above, there is the added dread of feeling trapped. Our commitment is tested, and in some cases, there does not appear to be any relief in sight. Any and all problems seem to be amplified, and every hurt feeling feels more acute.

We search aimlessly for joy in our life, and our actions are, more often than not, a cry for help. With time, we eventually shut down. We stop being who we are and sink further and further into the rabbit hole. Our life becomes an exercise in "going through the motions." We tell ourselves that maybe someday, things will turn around. We remind ourselves of our "for better or for worse" wedding vows, and we dredge on with the hope that things will be okay. We become self-absorbed out of desperation, and we wind up disliking the person we've become…which only adds to the downward spiral. As pathetic as it sounds, there are far too many couples out there who can relate to this feeling.

Sometimes, it is only one person feeling this way, and the other is totally unaware…and even happy. This, to me, sounds unfathomable. How could someone say they love someone else and be so oblivious to that other person's feelings? So much so that they don't even realize that something is wrong? It makes no sense to me, and I dare say it is not possible. What is more likely the case is they are in love with the situation they have created for themselves, not the person they are married to! As I mentioned before, when we do not better ourselves for the other person, we are not maintaining a forgiving spirit. We are simply taking advantage of the other person's good nature.

Many times, this is how a situation like this begins. This could very well be a case where one person's attention has shifted to reality, and they have lost focus of their relationship and their love. Or it could be a sign of something worse. Love longs for a forgiving spirit, and love will not survive without it… And it must be mutual. It seems fair to say that their ability to relate and share is in serious question. Without the ability to relate, mutuality is next to impossible to maintain. Even if they share common goals, without the ability to relate, there is no mutuality. When the lonely partner tries to confront the situation then, it often falls on deaf ears because their partner either can't relate or they don't want their self-endowed happiness to be jeopardized.

The ability to maintain this cry for help becomes harder and harder to do as the lonely partner sinks farther and farther into the rabbit hole and becomes more and more withdrawn! How can love survive something like this? Without a change of heart and a forgiving spirit, I am not sure that it can. Saying I am sorry means little to nothing without a change of heart. Core values must be reevaluated, and both reconciliation and forgiveness need to take place. With a change of heart, the hardest change of all, reconciliation can begin… and hopefully, with forgiveness and time, things will recover.

Sometimes both parties are feeling lonely, but neither one knows it…or perhaps both know it but neither one cares. This is a dire situation that requires immediate attention. Without reconciliation, the prognosis is not good. In these situations, both parties are withdrawn and entering their own rabbit holes. Everything is a chore, and there is nothing one person can do that will bring validation to the other.

The longer they wait, the more terminal the situation becomes. The ability to forgive, let alone reconcile, is next to impossible when both parties are hurting. Many times, intervention is required, and even that is no guarantee that love will survive. Their core values and their ability to relate are in serious question. Sometimes it is the lack of shared core values that is causing them not to be able to relate. How can love survive something like this? To be honest, I am not sure that it can or that it is even wanted by either party. If it were to happen, though, it would require both parties changing their hearts and realigning them with a shared core value that both can be committed to. Is it possible? Yes. But it would require all of their strength, patience, perseverance, and belief in each other…and the effort must be mutual. Recognizing the reality of the situation and the love that may still exist will help them make that decision.

In both of these scenarios, a change of heart is needed. In both cases, forgiveness and reconciliation are vital. When our core values are shared, anything is possible. If they are not, the chance for improvement is slim. When we are proficient at knowing who we are, when we have a healthy spirit of forgiveness, and when we relate to each other in a way that brings meaning to us, we are more prone to recovery. We have discussed the need to grow with each other and share each other's journey in light of those core values. When we grow together, we change…for the good. When we do not grow together, we still change but not necessarily in a good way.

This is where our friend mutuality comes into play yet again. Our relationships should never make us change to the point where we are not happy with ourselves... It should never change who we are. Wedding vows were never intended to bring us pain, only growth. The ironic thing is those of us who have spent time in that rabbit hole do not realize we have changed. We do not recognize how different we have become. All we know is that we are dissatisfied with ourselves. We blame ourselves for the situation we are in, and we constantly pray for answers that never seem to come. We cannot understand why we feel so lost, and we begin to question our own worth. The answers cannot be found until we recognize the problem. Many times, we cannot see the problem until we emerge into the light.

- Fight through challenges... Make it better.
- Take two steps back, forgive, and take three steps forward.
- See yourself through the eyes of the other...and grow.
- Look past pettiness...and seek understanding.
- Maintain a forgiving spirit. Keep it mutual.
- Cherish, appreciate, validate. Turn negatives to positives.

CHAPTER 5

Considering the Source

What an interesting trip to the rabbit hole that was! Talk about emerging into the light. The point to be made is the loving, healthy relationships we all long for cannot exist without two things: love and a relationship. That sounds obvious, but reality has little to do with either. Reality cannot take priority over our relationships. Reality is just a moment in time. Our commitment to each other is how we travel through time. Love is what brings meaning and worth to that commitment…and how we express it is our choice to make. It is this "worth" that I would like to spend some time reflecting on.

We have spent a lot of time in this nutshell, getting to know ourselves and exploring our relationship to each other in an effort to relate to love. As I mentioned at the start, love is so much more than our relationships. But our relationships are a good way to identify with love's significance in our lives. We have looked at our relationships from the fun side, the rewarding side, and the dark side. Maybe we should close out our look at the virtue of love by looking at the bright side of our relationships. The best way I know to do that is to consider the source of this entity we all have need of.

Before I lose some of you (if I have not done so already), I want to point out that what I am talking about is the source of this entity. The climate that we must be open to. This ideology can be labeled as anything you want. The important thing is that you acknowledge its existence. One thing is for sure, love is not a chemical reaction. It is not something that just happens based off of our mutual attraction. If that were true, then there would be no need for us to go any further. You have found your animal instinct, and you are done… Enjoy your reality, but you will need to call what you are experiencing something other than love…perhaps cohabitation would be a good word to use.

If it is love you are looking for, however, you need to look deeper. Love transcends reality. It goes beyond what we experience into a realm of other-centeredness. You can call it what you want, but anyone who has truly loved understands this connection to something universal…something greater than themselves. Haven't you ever had the experience of, when being in love, feeling like you could do anything? I am sure you have heard the expression "Love gives us wings." This is what I am talking about. This is the joy we bring to one another! Love elevates our game to a whole new level. We feed off each other to realize what we are truly capable of, so much so that we barely recognize ourselves!

A large majority of us grew up with a belief in God. We were taught that God is love. However true that message might be for us, many of us have learned to humanize the concept. Far too many of us have simply stopped believing… Such idealism does not exist. Perhaps we have come to that conclusion because all of those ideals are in direct contradiction to our own reality. Maybe we have found those ideals too difficult to fight for or live up to. Perhaps we believe in those ideals, we just don't believe in the so-called source. Perhaps we view it as childish. Regardless of our beliefs, I think it is fair to say that we can still acknowledge the existence of love in our lives… We can see the logic of being kind to each other and the reward that comes from caring. We know what it means to forgive, so everything we have discussed can still apply and hold meaning for anyone.

This is not about proving the existence of God per se. We will explore our need for faith a little later. For now, the point to be made is the love we share is bigger than we are as individuals. When we truly love one another, our relationships allow us to see the bigger picture with clarity and purpose.

It is important to point out, however, that those of us who do consider ourselves Christians have a perfect example of what love is in Jesus Christ. For us, God is the source of all love, and everything we have discussed gives meaning and lends credence to this, so much so that we are in awe of the gift that was given to us in His Son, Jesus. He is the epitome of forgiveness, intimacy, love, and sacrifice... He is love personified. Earlier, I talked about the virtues of faith, hope, and love. The greatest of these is love. I also mentioned that sacrifice was the proof of our love but clarified it by claiming that sacrifice could not happen without forgiveness. The basis for that claim is found here. One thing that I believe gets overlooked all too easily when it comes to Jesus is this... It is not by Christ's sacrifice that we are saved... It is through God's forgiveness that we are saved. His sacrifice is an act of forgiveness. "Father, forgive them, they know not what they do." If we love one another, we must be willing to forgive or there is no sacrifice... There is no proof of our love. Jesus paid the ultimate price to teach us this lesson. The ability to forgive and reconcile is at the core of every loving relationship.

I find it somewhat ironic that the vast majority of couples get married in a church, but so many of us treat it as just "the thing to do." Maybe it is just another way we try to start our relationships out as "ideal." We sanctify our union in God's presence and solidify our relationship with the binding words, "What God has joined, let no man put asunder," then proceed to drift farther and farther away from Him. It begs the question, "What did God really join? Was it God that did the joining or man?"

So many of us commit to each other, believing in the sanctity of marriage but fail to sanctify the relationship. I often wonder if this is yet another feeble attempt by us to manipulate love into some alternate reality. I wonder if this is why so many marriages fail. Remember, we cannot change love, love changes us!

I believe in the sanctity of marriage very much, but I do not buy into couples using it as a crutch to get what they want...consciously or unconsciously. Getting married in the church is not a "stamp of approval." It is a call to make this world a better place, by upholding what we believe in together. We do that by growing with and for each other and becoming better people. All this is done while maintaining our individuality...yet developing our mutuality. We learn to complement each other's strengths. We learn to change our hearts and think in terms of more than one person. That is what it is all about, and that is what makes love something bigger than you and me. The more we give to each other in the spirit of that love, the more we are able to give back…to everyone!

I also find it intriguing that couples who do allow God into their lives or who are committed to their core values, if you will, have a much higher rate of success. I truly believe that this happens because we start out believing in something greater than ourselves. The mere acknowledgment of that automatically allows us to see things in a different light. It lends itself to seeing the big picture and heightens our sense of self-awareness in relation to that picture… and each other. It grants us easy access to those core values. When we reach that level of awareness in a spirit of mutuality, it allows us to be godlike to each other…and to the rest of the world.

As I mentioned before, we are all on our own path to self-aware-ness. Understanding what makes us happy allows us to truly relate to each other in a way that brings meaning to the both of us. When core values are shared, it makes it so much easier to share and to grow together. For some of us, these core values exist but without the "God" connotation…and that is okay. But for Christians, having God as a resource grants many of us a wealth of values to experience and grow from together. How much more value is there when we seek God together as a couple?

I am not trying to say that everyone needs to believe in God in order to find love. What I am saying is that couples need to share the same ideology (core values) in order to relate to each other in a way that allows them to share. The journey we take together is the important thing as long as it allows us to grow in love. The more we can relate to each other in a spirit of understanding and share in a spirit of reconciliation, the easier it is for us to experience that growth… The more we are able to forgive, the more our love becomes unconditional. When we experience that level of love, we are more in tune with the big picture. We see things in a whole new light. When we Christians apply that to what Jesus taught us, we begin to see the truth behind the message. "If you can forgive one another, how much more will your heavenly Father forgive you?" Those of us whose relationships are built on this premise understand this. We begin to see that nothing is hard when it is done in a spirit of true love. We begin to understand what Jesus meant when He said, "My yoke is easy, my burden light."

I have a friend who reminds me of this message every day. She is relentless in her vocation…and her family. She works tireless hours to make sure everything under her watch functions like clockwork. I have often marveled at her fortitude and dedication. It matters not the time of day or day of the week. When she is called upon, she delivers. Many times, I have expressed concern for her health and well-being, wondering when she ever has time for herself. Invariably, her response to me is one of pure joy in her work. She loves what she does, and that is all there is to it. Her efforts are no effort at all… but rather an opportunity to continue doing what she loves to do the most! Perhaps you know someone just as dedicated. The point is, when we have love, we filter things differently, and what others would consider hardships, we consider blessings. And just like my dedicated friend and my brother who feels like the luckiest man on earth, we simply rejoice in the opportunity to love. That only comes from open hearts that are keenly aware of themselves…and others.

Many of us are not so "in tune" to have a vocation of such magnitude. Many of us find joy in just doing our good deed for the day. We have all had the experience of loving what we do, however small the deed might have been. The point to be made is when we do those good deeds, when we benefit others, we are filled with a positive feeling. This is a glimpse of what we can be to and for each other. A little act of kindness can go a long way toward making us feel better about ourselves. A little act of kindness is a very good way to change the way we view reality. Remember what we observed about young children at play? I rest my case.

When we are able to show kindness to each other, it allows us to give back. By the same token, when we take the time to recognize the kindness of others, it validates their worth to us and makes them feel better in return. This is a nice generic way to relate to each other and feel good about it…and the rewards are always positive! There is no greater reward in life than knowing you have made a difference in someone else's life…so taking the time to let someone know how much you appreciate their efforts is a great way to perpetuate that reward. I have often speculated that the reason many of us have a hard time realizing our worth is because the rest of us don't take the time to say "Thank you."

This is something I try to do regularly and especially when I am down or dejected about things. Not always successfully, but I try. I try to make a conscious effort to genuinely thank people when they make a difference. It is really quite amazing to see their reaction. When I do this during times when I find myself despairing, the rewards are twofold. It not only rewards their efforts, but it also allows me to take the time to appreciate life, enjoy creation, and cherish people…then I am able to look back on my own problems and smile. It is love that allows me to do this. In fact, it makes me wonder why I don't do it more often. A forgiving spirit opens our eyes to see things beyond our little world. If we are able to demonstrate this behavior to anyone on the street, imagine how much greater our efforts will be when we have the added blessing of relating to someone we can share our life with! That is the beauty of a loving relationship! The more we can support that in each other, the more we are able to give back.

I mentioned earlier that love was universal and all-encompassing. That it was the manner in which we channel it and who we choose to share it with that makes it unique and most vulnerable. When we have a vision of something greater than ourselves, when we have that ideology that allows us to remain focused on our efforts together, we are able to channel that love in a way that brings meaning to everyone as well as each other. Call it love, call it God, call it heaven, call it idealism, but there is no denying that when we are united in a common goal…a common value, the probability of success is so much greater! When we use that common value as a resource, our vulnerability becomes invulnerable! And when we are able to perpetuate that message in each other? I guess that is why they call it "heaven on earth."

By the same token, when we choose to internalize that love for our own benefit, when we try to channel it to fit our expectations, when we do not allow it to benefit others or each other, we are making love vulnerable and doomed to failure. But it isn't love that will be doomed to failure. It will be those of us who tried to force love to become something it is not. Therefore make yourself loveworthy... free of expectations, free of desires, free of personal wants. Love is none of these things! Love is not boastful; love is not rude. Love does not put on airs or have expectations. Love takes delight in others. It is patient and kind... Sound familiar? When we open ourselves to love through forgiveness, we realize the many ways that exist for love to find us. When we maintain a forgiving spirit, love will abide with us and stay with us... It always does.

I know all of this sounds a little over the top. I realize we are not living in a perfect world and that a lot of this is easier said than done. For many of us, it is a question of practicality. No matter how much we may agree with what is being said, inserting this philosophy into our current reality is pretty farfetched. I can't disagree with you. But as we take the time to insert some of these little gestures into our lives, our realities become brighter. When we take the time to relate to each other in a more meaningful way, our paths become clearer. When we allow ourselves to view life through the filter of the bigger picture, we begin to experience change for the better. When we discover someone to share that journey with, it becomes an opportunity to give back. Who needs a legacy when we have the opportunity to perfect life and perpetuate something as ideal as love? I ask again...

What more to life is there?
Than to grow in its light,
Fill it with love,
And give it back...
A more perfect entity.

- Let love transcend your reality. Elevate your game.
- Nurture your mutuality while maintaining your individuality.
- Take the time to say "Thank you!"
- Sanctify your relationship.

- Use God as a resource. Personalize His love.
- Seek growth and direction together... Give it back.
- Enjoy the gift of each other... Enjoy being loved.

CHAPTER 6

If Wishing Could Make It So

Just as love allows us to look beyond ourselves and see the bigger picture, hope and faith also give us a similar feeling. Very often it is the feeling of love that fills us with both. So what is the distinction between the three? How is hope and faith different from love? Likewise, what is the relationship between hope and faith? I have often wondered if perhaps they were the same thing. They do appear to have a lot of similarities. Does wishing and hoping for something make it come true? How does that work? Are there different levels of hope? When does hope turn into believing? Or is it belief that provides us with hope? These are the questions I found myself contemplating.

When you look up hope in the dictionary, you get the following definition, "The feeling that what is wanted can be had or that events will turn out for the best." Another definition I found was "To cherish a desire with anticipation, to want something to happen or be true." For Christians, we have yet another definition. "Hope is the conviction that no matter the circumstances, God's plans for our lives are for good and not for disaster."

It is a good thing we have these definitions to go by because I, for one, have always had a hard time truly understanding the virtue of hope. I have always regarded it as something mysterious and looked at it with a kind of generic meaning. Like many of us, I was unaware of what it truly meant to have hope, and I was blind to its significance in my life. We have probably all heard the saying that hope begins in the darkness. I suppose that makes sense in a lot of ways, but it still does not define the word for me or make it any more meaningful. Is hope so vague that it is whatever we want it to be, so long as we start in the dark? Still, in order to define it, we must know where to look…and maybe that is the mystery?

Hope is not defined through enlightened minds or found in textbooks… It is found in darkness…and its true meaning is defined with an open heart. It is the mystery of our own heart that allows us to realize hope's relevance in our lives. I guess I never really thought about it that way, and I am surprised it didn't occur to me to take that approach. We need to contemplate hope's meaning from the inside, not from the grand scheme of things. After all, it only makes sense that hope should flow from the ground up, from the inside out. Like a tree, it receives its life from within. How could we possibly understand what hope means to us looking at it from the outside?

I began to really concern myself with what hope means to me in my life and what it is that I truly hope for. I highly recommend this moment of meditation to everyone because I believe that the more time you spend reflecting on it, the more you begin to realize how much of a gift hope really is. As I reflected, I remembered the many ways hope was shown to me in my life, and I recalled the many times my attempts to trust in its meaning fell short of its true potential. The more I thought about it, the more I realized I was not giving hope enough credit. It certainly opened my eyes a bit. I decided I needed to change my view of hope and began to look at it in a whole new way. I did not dismiss it as something mysterious or view it as something generic any longer. I looked at it as something just as viable and just as real as any other virtue…just as real as love.

Armed with this realization, I took another look at those definitions to see which one made the most sense to me. I am not sure that any of them did a great job of defining the word for me, but they gave me a good place to start. The first definition didn't do a whole lot for me. It appeared to be a little wanting. It seemed to lack the passion that I feel is an integral part of the virtue of hope. The second definition made a little more sense to me. "To cherish a desire with anticipation…to want something to happen or be true." There are two keywords in that definition, "cherish" and "anticipation." To anticipate something implies expectation. To cherish something means to regard something as being dear to us…something of value (something true).

We could hope to win the lottery, but we would be foolish to "anticipate" it happening. We could hope for a lot of snow so school would be cancelled, but that would not be considered something we would hold dear to us…at least not something of value. So how could either of these be something we would really hope for? The Christian definition adds another keyword, "conviction," "a fixed or firm belief." I think these three words, *cherish, anticipation,* and *conviction* can go a long way in helping us shed some light on the topic of hope. What does it mean to hope?

Have you ever noticed how often we use the words *wish* and *hope* interchangeably? We substitute them for each other, all the time, without a second thought. Our objective in this chapter is to allow our definitions above to help us clarify the difference between hoping and wishing. Both wish and hope deal with desires, it would seem. The definition for wish demonstrates how closely related these words are… "To have a strong feeling of wanting something to happen or wanting to have something." As closely related as they might sound, it would seem there is distinction to be made. Wishes appear to be more whimsical and not grounded on anything substantial. "I wish I had a dime for every time I said that." "I wish the phone would stop ringing for five minutes."

Hope, on the other hand, seems to have more drive behind it. It appears to be grounded in reality or something concrete. "I hope your surgery goes well." "I hope the card I sent you brightened your day." I think that is an important point to remember as we move forward. With hope, there is direction. There is a common theme that we can all get behind and desire together. With hope, our desires are usually united… Let's hold on to that thought.

We really do use these two words (*hope* and *wish*) interchangeably so very often. So much so that I believe many of us have a hard time making the distinction…and there is a distinction to be made. There is more to hope than what we clarified above, and we should spend some time exploring this wonderful virtue. Hopefully, it will broaden our understanding. As with hope and wish, there are a couple of other words that are used interchangeably that could also use some clarification and understanding, "dream" and "vision."

In many ways, we can draw the same conclusions for these two words. One is founded on fantasy, the other on direction and focus. This lends itself to the following word association. Wish is to hope as dream is to vision. However we choose to use these terms, it is important that we understand what it is we are talking about. This *Webster's* dissertation is not meant to be an exercise in literacy or a chance to split hairs over what is supposedly real or not real. Rather, it is a chance for us to recognize the opportunity to contemplate and realize what hope really means in our lives and to understand its true value to us…and perhaps draw strength from it.

All too often, hope's meaning gets diluted out because of its association with wishing. It is my contention that it is for this reason we do not regard hope with as high of a value as we should. I think it is important, therefore, to differentiate between the two. Making sure we are on the same page with these terms should help to give us some direction…at least that is my theory. It is kind of like in the movie *E.T.* when E.T. was forced to separate himself from Elliott at the end of the movie. That is how intertwined these terms have become but how distinctly different they really are.

Of course, this whole mess started when we were children. "I wish I may, I wish I might, have the wish I wish tonight." Every Christmas, we would send our letters off to Santa, complete with our wish lists for the year. More often than not, at least some, if not most of our wishes would come true…as "Santa's helpers" would always be listening. Of course, why wouldn't we believe that wishes come true? It seems that a child can wish for just about anything, and there is a good chance it will happen. It is too bad we have to lose that innocence. But as Paul reminds us in Scripture, "When I was a child, I talked like a child, I thought like a child, I reasoned like a child. When I became a man, I put the ways of the childhood behind me."

No offense to Paul, but I'm not so sure I would be so quick to dismiss childhood. Still he makes a valid point. The way we view our world has to have an element of maturity to it. We have to grow in our understanding of our own existence as well as our relationship with others and with God. It is only right that as we mature, we view the world through reason and careful reflection. That can only be accomplished through adult rationalization, right?

It is during the course of these discoveries that we begin to seek clarity and revelation about life and what has meaning and true value to us. It is during these discoveries that we begin to search and long for those things that validate our worth…and bring us to a broader understanding. We begin to hope. We hope for ourselves, for our children, for all mankind. We begin to look forward to brighter days, and we face the future with anticipation of what lies ahead…not unlike a child waiting for Christmas. Hope, by its very nature, infers anticipation, joy, and even excitement! That doesn't mean we can't be adults about it. It poses the question then, is the difference between wishing and hoping just a matter of maturity?

One of my favorite Disney characters has always been Jiminy Cricket. In a world of fantasy, he was the voice of reason. He was always depicted as the voice of logic… The little voice inside the heads of the other characters…their conscience, if you will. His greatest work was with Pinocchio, the puppet who became a boy. Not for himself but as a result of the vision and undying hope of Geppetto, the puppet master who had no son of his own. Pinocchio spends the entire movie trying to prove his self to be brave, truthful, and unselfish, so as to earn the right to become a human boy…all under the guidance of Jiminy Cricket. Their search is filled with adventure, mischief…and discovery. Sounds a lot like real life, yes? Fantasy or not, we can all identify with the struggles of discovering who we are. Of course, one of the best Disney songs of all time came out of that movie, "When You Wish Upon a Star." One of my favorite lines from that song is the following:

> When your heart is in a dream, no request is too extreme.
> When you wish upon a star, your dreams come true.

That song taught a generation how to hope, and it spoke to the child in all of us! Fantasy or not, it taught us a valuable lesson about what it means to hope…or at least to dream. The songwriters give us a perfect example, however, of how intertwined these concepts are as they use the words "wish" and "dream" in these verses.

I realize we are talking about a fictional movie, but this song poses all kinds of questions which demonstrate my point. If your heart is truly into something, would that qualify as a wish or a hope? A dream or a vision? If your dream comes true, is it still a dream or was it more likely a vision? Can dreams really come true? Can wishing make it so? Or if something like that were to happen, would it be considered more like a coincidence? There are some very interesting insights to be made here. Maybe we cannot make wishes come true until we filter it through hope. Maybe dreams only come true when we "envision" them happening. Maybe hope IS vision!

It can get convoluted. It is not easy to differentiate sometimes. Even the best of us get it mixed up. Martin Luther King Jr. may have had a dream, but I would dare say his dream was more like a vision, wouldn't you agree?

Hope, as it turns out, is a vital part of our existence. We have all heard the expression of "being without hope," but I wonder if any of us have truly experienced even a taste of what that really means or feels like. Hope is an essential part of our existence because it challenges us and allows us to always look forward. No one has ever hoped for past events. If we were truly void of hope, we would be lost and without choice. That, in and of itself, should have significant meaning to us. As relevant as that insight might be, however, we still do not give hope it's just due. We continue to use it as a common term to indicate our every desire. We even "hope against hope" in some instances…which, if you think about it, is an oxymoron, if ever I've heard one. All of this downplays the potential and significance of true hope in our lives. It is as if we like having it around, but we don't really believe in it. We use it as just another expression of want…like wishing. I think it is time we change that mentality.

⬤ Hope infers cherishing and anticipation. Be careful what you wish for.

- Hope may begin in darkness, but its meaning can only be found within.
- Don't overlook hope's significance. Without it, we would be without choice.
- Filter your wishes through hope. Allow your dreams to become vision.

CHAPTER 7

The Color of Hope

What does hope look like? How do we recognize it in our lives? As with most things, the simplest place to look for it is in creation. Rainbows are often used as a symbol of hope. Likewise, spring has always been depicted as the season of hope, the color of green, the promise of new life. Not to be a downer or anything, but since we are defining hope through darkness, shouldn't winter be the season of hope? Isn't it the bleakness of winter that compels us to look forward to brighter days ahead? Spring is more like the fulfillment of that hope, isn't it? Regardless, the message is the same. We cherish with anticipation the coming of warmth and new life. It is something we are confident will come because of our experience and knowledge, and we look forward to it every year. We have the reality of the season in front of us to give us something to look forward to. Let me say that again…we have confidence in its arrival, and we have the reality of the season in front of us to look forward to.

As I mentioned before, hope infers anticipation, joy, and excitement. We experience these feelings of encouragement every spring and throughout the year. They are a constant reminder to us of how important these events are. We acknowledge the significance of these events in our lives, and we even become passionate about their arrival. Who doesn't get excited about Christmas coming? The first snowfall of the season? Or that first refreshing summer breeze that makes our hearts want to do everything? I know it is a simple example, but it is an easy way to demonstrate how hope makes us feel. As these events come to pass in our lives, we learn that we must prepare ourselves for their arrival so we will be ready to enjoy them fully. Each season brings new challenges, and we take on those challenges with anticipation and excitement for what lies ahead.

Hope allows us to face these obstacles with confidence. Hope fills us and gives us a feeling of ownership and accountability to do what is necessary. Sometimes those challenges require sacrifices on our part, but we do them willingly because we know that what lies ahead is worth the effort. Think of all the things we do, year in and year out, to prepare ourselves and our homes for each season, each Christmas, each holiday. Think of all the excitement and anticipation that goes into our vacations and celebrations. These are small but very real examples of hope and what we are willing to do to prepare for what we know is coming. This much excitement over something so small makes you wonder how exciting things of a greater magnitude could be… Food for thought.

Spring is full of new life, the days are longer, and temperatures are warmer. We have St. Patrick's Day, Mother's Day, and Easter to celebrate! It is no accident that we celebrate Easter with the arrival of the vernal equinox every year. Leading into Easter, we Catholics (and other denominations) have the season of Lent. It is a season of preparation as we get ready for the most sacred liturgical event of the year, Jesus's resurrection. We look at Lent as a time of repentance and a time of almsgiving, of sacrifice and prayer. There is a lot to be said for this. Those of us who take this season seriously truly understand the significance of this time for self-discovery and reflection. It is a reminder to us all of how lost we are without hope. Still I have often wondered why we do not take more time to emphasize hope this time of year.

For reasons I mentioned above, hope beckons us to a life of sacrifice and preparation, just as much as the traditional Lenten rituals do. Why not celebrate it as a season of renewal as well as a season of repentance? Present it as a season of fulfillment and community as well as one of self-discipline. In many ways, they briefly touch on this concept, but I wish they would emphasize it even more. After all, what do we have to be more hopeful for than the resurrection of our Savior? Just like spring, we look forward to Easter every year, and we know it is coming. It is an opportunity for us to cherish with anticipation rather than repent with humility…even though both are needed.

Hope is often referred to as a light at the end of the tunnel…a beacon of light, if you will, to light the way. I think that is a good analogy, but I would also like to think of that light as something that shines through us…if we let it. All we need to do is open the door. One thing is for certain, hope's light remains bright and constant. What this means then is the darker the place, the brighter that light appears. This is why we hear the phrase "Hope is found when things are darkest." We have all had the experience of walking into a dark room. It takes a while for our eyes to adjust. The darker the room, the longer it takes to adjust, and in total darkness, we do not see anything. The slightest glimmer of light is then magnified. That is the beauty of hope!

Even in our darkest moments, the light of hope shines for us to see… The darker the moment, the stronger the signal. The hardest part is getting out of our own way long enough to take notice of it. When we are in the midst of these dark moments, it is hard not to be self-absorbed. Taking notice of hope's message is a lot harder than one might think. Oftentimes it is not until we look beyond ourselves that we begin to notice that the light even exists. Even still, hope remains constant. Those who are ready and open to it seek its calling. Those who are not remain in the dark. Another way to look at this is those who have been in that dark room are able to see light that those new to the darkness cannot see… "Those who dwell in darkness have seen a great light."

As I mentioned earlier, hope keeps us looking forward. That is easier said than done when we are consumed with the present. When we do not allow ourselves to move forward, we become stagnant and run the risk of losing our way. I think some of us are reluctant to move forward, at times, for fear of losing what we have. I know I have fallen victim to this mindset on more than one occasion. But if we walk in the light of hope, we should always be happy to move forward with the understanding that moving forward does not necessarily imply change. Sometimes it only means improving what is already there. Some of us are more willing to take those steps than others. Some hit the door running, some walk with more caution. Some haven't left the porch yet, and some haven't even opened the door.

The beautiful thing is hope waits patiently for us. The light keeps beckoning, and it is ready for us when we decide to take our first steps forward... It is always there for us to see. As we begin to move forward, things start to become brighter and clearer. But not until we move... And it is up to us to take those steps. Hope is like taking a trip without a map. It is like taking a hike in the deep woods with no trail and no compass. But it is a trip worth taking and a hike full of wonder.

Hope allows us to take those steps with anticipation rather than reluctance... With excitement rather than fear. Have you ever done something you really didn't want to do? How many of us have put off going to the dentist or the doctor? Now compare that to something you have looked forward to doing...a movie you have been dying to see or a vacation you have been planning for months. That is the kind of excitement a life of hope brings to us. That is the spring hope puts into our step.

That same kind of vitality and excitement must have taken place in ancient times when "Jesus came to bring hope to the sinners." We hear this phrase a lot, but I am not sure we understand how profound a message it really was back in the time of Jesus. When we hear it, we probably think, *Okay, He gave them something to look forward to*, with the same kind of generic lackluster perception that we view hope today.

But let's think about this for a moment. Given everything we just talked about, can you imagine the gift that was given? At the time of Jesus, there was no real hope for the sinner...there was no anticipation or excitement. You were in or you were out. The punishment fit the crime, and there was little room for forgiveness. "An eye for an eye" was the adage of the times. As if this weren't enough, during the time of Jesus, any afflictions you might have been dealt were considered by many to be a result of some sin you must have committed! You were guilty, even if you were innocent!

If you want to put this in perspective, imagine yourself in this period in time. Imagine all of your own transgressions which are nowadays tolerated and put them in a society with zero tolerance. How many of us would be out on the street, stripped of our dignity? How many of us would be branded as harlots or thieves or unclean? Now imagine not being allowed to make amends for those sins and prove yourself trustworthy ever again. You are forevermore considered an outcast. Likewise, consider yourself or others you may know and love who are burdened with birth defects or disabilities. Imagine them being forgotten and isolated…being branded as evil and guilty by association with no recourse for a semblance of a normal life, let alone help with their afflictions.

Make no mistake about it, these were very dark times! Remember, the darker the times, the brighter the signal… Jesus's light of hope must have shown bright indeed! Can you imagine the excitement that was generated upon hearing the news of Jesus's arrival? Can you imagine the thrill they would have…we would have…knowing we might have a second chance at life?

That is how great hope is! That is how we should be viewing hope today! The great irony of the whole thing is Jesus still brings hope to the sinner…and I would dare say we are in need of it more now than ever! We view those ancient times as primitive and dark, never thinking for a second that perhaps the times we are living in today may be even darker. How many of us are too consumed with the present to see that? I know I have fallen into this trap many, many times myself. In a world of tolerance and excess, hope's light continues to burn, but we do not realize how dark it really is and fail to seek hope's direction.

The thing we fail to realize is that just as in the dark room the light appears brighter, then it is also true that in a lighter room, the harder it is to see that same true light. Is it any wonder hope's meaning has become so diluted? In many ways, the people in ancient times had it easy…at least they didn't have as many lights to choose from. They did not have as many things distracting them from the truth.

Perhaps it is for this reason that Jesus came to us when He did. The greatest story ever told came at a time when the greatest lessons were there to be learned and have the most profound impact. I pray our journeys will always bring us to that same realization and that we will allow ourselves to be open to that truth.

Because Jesus came when He did, we have great examples of God's life-giving hope on earth…like in the parable of the cripple whose sins Jesus forgave. Jesus was rebuked for forgiving his sins. Jesus retorted and said, "Which of these is easier to say? 'Your sins are forgiven you' or 'Rise and walk home'? So that you may know that the son of man has the power to forgive sins…"

And Jesus proceeds to heal the lame man. Can you imagine the hope that was given that cripple? He was given a chance to live a full life again…inside and out! Do you know what part of that story strikes me the most? The very last line… "So that you may know that the son of man has the power to forgive sins." What a revelation that must have been to the people of the time, and yes, to people even today! So much power has been bestowed upon us in His name, but we are too afraid to use it… Why?

Ah my favorite unsung virtue, forgiveness. We have the power to forgive each other. What a concept! It may very well be the most underutilized and most powerful weapon we humans have. The only way to prove me wrong is to try it out and see. Many of us hesitate to do this because two things have to happen before forgiveness can take place… We have to be wronged and we have to admit we are wrong. But this is exactly where the power resides. This is where the magic begins. When we forgive, we give hope. When we are forgiven, we feel hope. We anticipate and cherish the best in each other as a sign of that hope. Maybe the color of hope isn't green at all…maybe it is red…the color of love. Regardless, there is no denying that we have an endless supply of hope available to us through forgiveness.

When we act in the name of what is right, when we follow our conscience, when we act for the greater good, we give hope to each other. Once we do that, hope has now become personalized. Hope is no longer a mystery. Hope is no longer out there…it is in here. Bringing hope to each other is our calling. It is the gift we bring to one another. We see it over and over. Strangers helping strangers… Friends taking care of friends… Loved ones helping other family members through tough times…being there for each other during times of loss. What a blessing we have in one other!

My parents were very good role models for me. Everything I needed to know about faith and hope I could find somewhere in their example…even if my willingness to see those examples came at a later time in my life. My father was a pillar of faith in many respects. He was very good at articulating his beliefs and providing us with guidance. My mother was an expert at bringing all of those things to life. Dad talked about it. Mom lived it. My mother gave me countless examples of how we give hope to others as I was growing up.

One of the stories I want to share with you was just one small but profound act on her part and something I did not hear about until much later in my life from someone entirely unrelated. If not for them, I would have never known of its occurrence, so I am eternally grateful. It is a great example of giving hope to one another. Isn't it amazing how one small act of kindness can go unnoticed to some but mean so much to others? So much so that its impact remains strong for so many years? This story has to do with how I received my name.

I come from a large family. I was the fourteenth of fifteen children born to my parents…and twelve of us were boys! Needless to say, my parents were running out of options for names by the time I came around. As fate would have it, the blessed day for my arrival was close at hand, and my mother was taken to the hospital. Still a name had not been chosen. My mother shared a room with another woman who was also set to deliver at any moment. During the course of their stay together, my mother and this woman had the opportunity to get to know each other. Unlike nowadays, there was no "ship them in and ship them out" when it came to childbirth, and private birthing rooms were unheard of. Women were in the hospital for up to a week or even longer before being discharged. It just so happened that my mother's roommate's delivery resulted in a stillbirth. My mother had experienced a stillbirth of her own several years before. You can imagine the grief and the sorrow this woman and, for that matter, both women must have experienced and shared.

My mother, in midst of all of this sorrow, graciously asked her if it would be okay if she could use the name she was using for her son to name me. Her roommate was touched and consented. And that is how I received my name. As I later found out, this woman kept track of me throughout my life from that day forward…quietly celebrating my little victories and rejoicing in my various accomplishments. I had become a way for her to keep the memory of her son alive, all because of the hope my mother had given her during a very dark moment in her life.

This may be viewed as just a small example in the grand scheme of things, but that is the point. Our acts of hope do not have to be grand gestures…they just need to happen. One small act can have a significant impact, just as it did for my mother's roommate. My mother did what she felt was right. It made sense to her, and she acted on it. She did that a lot as you will later see. The point is this is a good example of how hope can become personalized. Hope has now become symbolized by a different kind of rainbow…a rainbow of the heart. A rainbow that only shows itself when hearts are shared. Spring is now more than just the season of hope. It is now the symbol of a timeless season…the endless springs that live in each of us.

I am reminded of a children's story I wrote a while back. I would like to share with you. It is a fictional representation of the same message. I share it with you, if for no other reason than for my own enjoyment. It is about a butterfly named Norm.

There once was a butterfly named Norm. One day in the meadow after a brief shower, Norm noticed a colorful rainbow in the sky. *How beautiful,* Norm thought to himself. *Those colors are even prettier than mine! I must find out where this is coming from.* Norm knew that the end of the rainbow looked very far away, but he was determined to find the answer to his quest. Norm started on his way… After a short while, Norm came across a bunny that had stopped along the edge of the meadow to partake of some of the green vegetation that was growing there. The bunny's name was Barry. He had one gold tooth and, much to Norm's surprise, was wearing glasses.

Norm had never seen a bunny with glasses before and couldn't help but stop to ask the bunny about his condition. Norm sat on a nearby flower and most respectfully asked Barry why he was wearing glasses. Barry explained that all his life, he had been eating peas, and because he did not have enough carrots in his diet, he wasn't able to see as well as he should. Barry was in search of these carrots so that he could regain his eyesight and give up peas for good! Barry asked where Norm was headed in such a hurry. Norm told Barry that he was chasing the rainbow to see what made the beautiful colors. Barry noticed that the rainbow was already starting to fade and told Norm he'd better hurry. Norm looked up, and sure enough, just as Barry had said, the colors were not as bright as they once were.

"I must leave you now, my new friend. I know that this rainbow ends just beyond these trees, and I must hurry before it goes away." Norm promised Barry he would keep an eye out for any carrot patches along the way. He flew away as Barry was wishing him luck.

Luck is just what Norm needed. He was so afraid he would not make the end of the rainbow in time. Through the trees he flew as fast as he could. He only stopped briefly to ask a wandering turtle for directions. The turtle, whose name was Timothy, was glad to help and told Norm that he heard others say, "If you followed this pipe that the humans have made, it would sometimes lead to a wonderful place." He had never seen it himself but knew that it was true.

This gave Norm even more motivation to reach his destination. On and on he flew. Finally, just when Norm thought he was too late, just as he was afraid the light had gone out, he came upon a clearing. In the clearing, Norm couldn't believe what he was seeing! There before him were all the colors of the rainbow, shining as brightly as before. They seemed to be coming from two humans who were in the clearing. They looked to be the best of friends, and they were sharing with each other as they leaned against the pipe that the turtle had told him about. What a special feeling that must be. Norm thought to himself, *To generate that much color, warmth, and beauty, it must be coming from their hearts.*

Norm learned a valuable lesson that day. And though his trip turned out to be different than he ever dreamed possible, he knew his trip was not wasted. Rainbows, he realized, are not something to be looked at but rather something to be made. Rainbows are the colors of the heart, and it only gets to come out when it is shared. Norm knew the secret of making rainbows and couldn't wait to go back to his new friends to tell them what he found.

They say that the forest floor turned a lot brighter in the days ahead. There were reports of beautiful colors of light shining through the trees. Thanks to Norm, the butterfly, Barry, found his carrot patch, Timothy got to finally see the rainbow, and the whole world was just a brighter place to be. The end.

Whether it is a fictional animal character, my own mother, or even Jesus, the point is hope does not only infer excitement, anticipation, and joy…it infers action as well. When we give hope the opportunity to show itself, it shines every time...and it shines through us. Forgiveness opens the door for the exchange of that hope in each other. Hope is a journey. It is the promise of a destination. It is not a roadmap on how to get there. Hope beckons, it does not reach out. We have each other for that... The choice is ours to make. It is our choice to help...it is our choice to accept. This is where our hope becomes united. When we are united, it is easier to open that door. When we are united, it is easier to take that step off the porch... Everything is easier when we are doing it together. We need to look for hope in our lives like we look for love.

Hope, like love, is never self-serving and invariably benefits everyone. We rarely look for hope, however. I am not exactly sure why that is. Maybe it is because we are too busy looking for love all of the time. Maybe we view it as a pipedream. Maybe we just don't see the reward in it and don't see the point in making the effort. Maybe it is because we do not look at hope as something to be shared. I can relate to that reasoning. Hope can be a very personal thing for us. But hope, like every other virtue, is best served shared. It could be we do not know enough about hope to know what to even look for. Maybe that is the problem? Could it be that our ability to hope is weak? As weak as our faith, perhaps?

- Take ownership of things hoped for. Do what you can to prepare.
- Hope infers anticipation, joy, excitement...and action.
- Do not consume yourself with the present. Move forward in hope.
- Hope, like love, is best served shared.
- Forgive and give hope. Be forgiven and receive hope.

CHAPTER 8

Giving Our Hopes a Chance

When I was in college, I was part of a new "team" approach to teaching Sunday school. We had a lot of fun relating to our eighth-grade classes, and for the most part, I would have to say that the program was a big success. I remember a little story we used to tell our classes each year to bring home the message of community. Perhaps you may have heard it. It goes like this:

> In the land of WE-dom, a baby "i" was born.
> One day, all the WE's of the "dom" gathered around and said together, "Hi, i."
> And from that day forward, little i grew into a capital fellow (I).

The message was obvious. Without each other, we do not grow as we should. The gift we are to one another is what allows us to be a part of something special and universal. Ignoring each other, therefore, has the opposite effect. Therefore "Love one another as I have loved you." And not just certain people...all people.

When we act from the heart, we act for the greater good. When we act from the heart, it is nearly impossible to be thinking of ourselves. This is where our virtues live. When we allow ourselves to filter our actions through these virtues, then everything we do becomes a little more enlightened. So the question becomes...where is your heart? The answer to that question is not an easy one if we really take the time to answer it truthfully. Sometimes there is a lot of darkness we have to sort through before we get to the answer to that question. It is a good thing our virtues are there waiting for us to show us the way.

When we allow ourselves to take this journey through our own consciousness, we discover what is really important to us. By acting on those values, we are giving ourselves the opportunity to be the best we can be... We have a better understanding of what to cherish and anticipate in our lives... We are giving our hopes a chance. Hope then raises our spirits and allows us to see ourselves as something greater than who we are. We give our hopes a chance by taking action in a way that validates hope's meaning to us.

When we take the time to look at hope as a virtue and not a wish, we begin to see the logic of it all. When we hope, it should come from the heart. After all, when it is all said and done, we are all children of the same spirit. Remember that thought I wanted you to hold on to from an earlier chapter? This is why I say hope is something we can all get behind. Whether it is two or twenty or twenty million, the reasons for our hopes are usually united. Sometimes it is only a matter of getting others to see it too. When we act from the heart, getting others on board is a much easier thing to do.

This is where I believe our definitions could put things in perspective for us. It only makes sense to me that combining our three words would send a very powerful message of what the true meaning of hope should be! When we *cherish* with *anticipation* a *conviction*, it carries a lot more weight, and I dare say redefines the word for us! For it is the passion of cherishing and the will of anticipation that allows hope to have true meaning for us in the first place! That is the positive energy that gives us something to look forward to. When what we are looking forward to is a fixed or firm belief (a conviction), it makes hope something special...something worthy of our respect and even reverence. As we discussed previously, it gives us accountability and ownership to do what is necessary to bring about change for the good. It gives us the optimism and fortitude to look forward to what we know is coming. Maybe hope really is vision!

I made a reference to Martin Luther King Jr. earlier. He is a perfect example of this! Martin Luther King Jr.'s "dream" was a value he held close (cherished) and looked forward to with expectation (anticipation). He inspired a generation to look into their hearts and envision a world of equality and peace (a conviction). He, as much as anyone, stood against the greed and injustice of the time…and thank God he did! The movement he inspired is still with us today…and it has changed the world! His hope for the future is still being realized. There is a reason he is revered by so many. He did not act for himself, he acted from the heart. He filtered his actions through his values, and his hopes were shared by so many of us because they came from the same spirit. Dr. King was well-known for his speeches and many quotes. You see them everywhere. He was a prolific speaker, and his words were always moving and stirred the soul. One of my favorite MLK quotes is this one:

> I believe that unarmed truth and uncon-
> ditional love will have the final word in reality.
> That is why right, temporarily defeated is stron-
> ger than evil triumphant.

I must say, the man did have a way with words. His words united a whole generation in a message of hope. With time, those hopes are becoming reality. What allowed his hopes to become realized? His speeches invariably pitted good against evil, peace against violence. It spoke to the greater good. We all bought into his message because he spoke of ideals that made sense to us. Our desires became united. Our ownership and commitment to those ideals brought about change and allowed his hope…our hope to become reality.

This is where it gets really good because there is a valuable lesson to be learned here… His hope, our hope is becoming reality, why? It is more than because we are united. There are all kinds of united causes out there that do not always have the best interest of everyone at heart. It is more than because it sounds like a good idea. Those are a dime a dozen. It is because his dream…his vision was founded in truth. I have come to believe that this is the quintessential ingredient that comprises hope. If there is not an element of truth in the picture, then there can be no hope. I believe this is the definitive qualifier that separates hope from a wish, and I am surprised it is not mentioned in our definitions above.

With this knowledge, if what I am saying has any merit, it can be stated then that true hope cannot be based on a false premise. Therefore hope cannot exist without a purpose. Hope is a real entity that has a real outcome because it is founded on a fundamental truth. In Hebrews we read "Faith is the assurance of things hoped for." As true as that may be, I would like to do it one better. Perhaps hope is not just our desire for faith, but rather the expression of faith itself? Just as the anticipation of the approaching season causes us to prepare for its coming, maybe hope is our way of preparing ourselves for the truth. Just as forgiveness is the expression and ultimate proof of our love, perhaps hope is the expression and proof of our faith. What if hope is really faith in action? Our faith is so very weak, how would we know? Our faith is so weak it almost feels like a dream or a wish. We all hope we have faith… Maybe it is time we start believing we do and start hoping that we can find a way to express that faith to others… And by hoping, I mean start preparing a way to take action. Who knows? Maybe we'll even move some mountains along the way. All we need is a mustard seed's worth, right?

Whether I am right or wrong, it doesn't really matter, but it does stimulate some thought, does it not? The point remains, we cannot possess hope and be idle. In one capacity or another, we are moving toward something, and that is the point to be made. So many times, we hope for something as a declaration of defeat. A last resort, if you will… We hoped for it now it is out of our hands. Hoping for something is just the first step. It is not the end…it is the beginning. The only declaration we should be making is to ourselves; that we are going to filter our actions through this newfound hope from now on because it is based on truth, and it is for the greater good.

Obviously, there are few like Dr. King out there. But our efforts do not have to be so landmark. Our efforts can be as simple as showing kindness to a stranger or giving a smile to the lonely. I do believe, however, that there is an element of truth that must be reconciled within each of us before we can obtain hope (or give it). If we can learn to ask ourselves that question (where is the truth in what I want?) each time we desire something, I think we could really help ourselves find true hope…and justify our needs. If we can filter our desires through the reality of that truth, then maybe our hopes will never be in vain.

As I stated, Dr. King always preached a message of peace over violence. His quote above bears this out very nicely. That quote put us in a race against evil, and he predicted the outcome…at least he knew what horse to not bet on. When it is all said and done, evil will never win. Evil, injustice, prejudice, bias, racism, and even complacency will always bring up the rear. Justice, peace, goodness, kindness, and forgiveness will always be among the leaders. I believe the winner, however, will always be truth.

When you find something to be true, you want to spread the word. Libraries and universities are built and thrive on this very premise. The newer the information, the more excitement there is. We see this everywhere from the lowest form of gossip to the latest breaking headline news. Each new discovery brings a barrage of questions and hypotheses to validate its legitimacy. Once proven, it is celebrated, welcomed, and absorbed as part of the norm. Every major development in human history has been made in this way. How do you think these truths were discovered? How much thought and effort had to go into these revelations? How much hope? When Einstein discovered the theory of relativity, do you think he said, "Gee, I hope that's right" and gave up on it? No, he took action to prove his theory and unraveled a scientific truth for us. If we believe in a truth, we work toward that truth until it is realized. There is only one truth, but it manifests itself in a multitude of different ways. Find the truth in each day that you enter and lend credence to it with your own voice. Do that, and we give our hopes a chance!

- Seek enlightenment… Where is your heart?
- Cherish with anticipation your conviction. Hope is vision.
- Look for the truth in what you desire and find true hope.
- Act from the heart…personalize hope…and give your hopes a chance.

CHAPTER 9

Hand in Glove

So what is the relationship between faith and hope? Are they related or are they separate entities? If we listen to me, I guess they are related. But since I am a blind man, all I am left with is a lot of speculation and reflection. I can't help but believe they are very much related, though. To these eyes, it only makes sense that they go hand in hand. Both virtues are steeped in truth (though you will never hear anyone define it that way). If you look for the definition of faith, you often find the word *trust*. You also find the word *conviction* again. Perhaps I am being presumptuous (it wouldn't be the first time).

Hope is defined as wanting something to be true. Faith is defined as complete trust that something is true but neither of them state that they are based on truth. Faith is defined as believing in what we cannot see. Hope is the desire that what we are not seeing is true. So answer me this, if what we are not seeing is not really there and what we are hoping to be true is not really true, what need do we have of faith and hope? Why would we do that to ourselves? Why would Jesus even have perpetuated such a notion? Of course, it is okay to have faith that we will have a spring next year and hope for warmer weather. We have the luxury of knowing these things happen every year. Halley's Comet only come's once every seventy-five years, but we have faith and hope it is coming. There are cosmic events that have not happened in a millennium, but we know they took place and will happen again. Are you getting my point? We may not be privy to it in our lifetime, but it doesn't make it any less true.

For me to claim that hope and faith are founded in truth may be a little bold, but not if you look at it from the dark. Forgive the "pun-like" analogy, but it is as clear as night and day. I will try to make that point a little later. For now, the relationship between the two is where I would like to focus my attention. I titled this chapter "Hand in Glove," and that is pretty much how I see their relationship. They complement each other so well and so often that it is hard sometimes to tell which is being demonstrated. I have another great example of this from where else? My mother.

My mother and father were very diligent about making every Christmas special in their own way when I was growing up. Being a part of it was my gift…remembering that it was better to give than to receive. We were a family of simple means, and with such a large family, my parents certainly knew how to stretch a dollar. Every year, my parents would prepare well in advance for the holidays using their creative gifts to shower us with abundant blessing. My dad developed a knack for wine making over the years. I and my some of my brothers used to help him gather his crop every year. He experimented with all kinds. He was a perfect example of making lemonade out of lemons. Our neighborhood would be overrun with dandelions every spring. Rather than curse them and battle them every year, he would send us out to pick every blossom we could find so he could make dandelion wine. He also made rhubarb wine, gooseberry wine, blackberry wine, the list went on. This had become quite the treat for my older siblings (and their spouses) every Christmas.

My mother was quite the baker and candymaker. Every holiday, our pantry would be filled with every delicacy imaginable, and believe me, we enjoyed every bite. Those of us at home were strictly forbidden to partake of these treats until our sibling visitors and their children arrived, but we were excellent at stealthy maneuvers to sneak a piece of what was rightfully ours. Mom was also very big into crocheting and would begin as early as March to get things done in time for Christmas. For the grandchildren, it might be dolls or slippers, for the adults, it might be hot pads or place mats.

Being one of the youngest, most of my older siblings were grown and married, so my parents' efforts were, more often than not, concentrated on the married siblings and their grandchildren. Those of us still at home were almost considered the outsiders when it came to Christmas. Let's just say all of their homemade efforts were meant for the married couples, not us, except for the candy, of course.

One particular year, when I was just out of college, I remember my mother made an afghan for each sibling that was not living at home. They were beautiful! They were of various colors and designs, all homemade and all made with the loving perfection of a woman who knew her craft. I knew all too well the countless hours she put into making these works of art as it took her the entire year to complete them. I was very jealous of my siblings since, being at home, I was not to receive one. After all, what would she do with an additional afghan or two lying around the house? Regardless, I made my wishes known to her that I wanted one which I could call my own, and I kept reminding her of it for several years thereafter. I would never let her forget how important it was to me to have one. Finally, after years of waiting, I received an afghan from my mother. I was thrilled! It was the best present I ever remember getting from her, and I cherished it dearly.

Shortly thereafter, our family was hit with the sad news that my brother had passed away at the age of forty-two. It was a hard time for all of us and my mother especially. Later that same year, his son, my nephew, came to visit his grandma. During the course of his visit, he made a comment to her that he admired her handiwork with the afghan and wished he had one. Without a single moment's hesitation, she told him that he could have mine and asked me to go upstairs and get it off my bed and bring it down for him. I was in shock! All I could do was stare at her. My mouth had to be hanging open, I am sure. She quietly assured me she would make me another one. This, of course, fell on deaf ears as I was quietly assuring myself that something would happen, and I would never see another one again!

I did not see it at the time, but she was giving my nephew hope that day and simultaneously teaching me a valuable lesson on what it meant to have faith. She was giving my nephew a piece of home and lifting his spirits at a time when his spirit needed it. At the same time, she was showing faith in me that I would comply with her wishes. I was giving her hope that I would be okay with it, and I was having faith in her that she would be true to her word. I was giving my nephew hope in doing the right thing, and he was showing me the reward of having faith in me. I could have argued and stood my ground on the matter. Believe me, the thought crossed my mind. As much as I may have understood her reasoning, this was simply asking too much.

Didn't she realize how long I had waited for this and how much it meant to me? And now she is asking me to just hand it over? All of a sudden, I am reminded of the Bible story when Abraham was asked to sacrifice Isaac. Not that dramatic, I know, but I am still reminded of it. Regardless, there was no arguing with pure goodness (which my mother was). I very quietly, albeit reluctantly, did as she requested. Looking back, I am very grateful I did not cause a scene about it. I think my mother was aware of the sacrifice I was making. I only had to wait a few months before I received my replacement. It was bigger and more beautiful than the last, and I have it with me to this day. Believe me, it has not been handled with kid gloves either. It has lasted through twenty-three years of marriage, three children, five dogs, three cats, and it still looks as beautiful as the day I received it. It is close to forty years old now and still looks amazing.

There is a part of me that likes to think that its buoyant great condition is a blessing bestowed upon me from above as a reward for my obedience and a way for my mother to be a part of my life forever. There are times when I take solace in that thought. I just hope she doesn't find out about the candy.

Maybe hope isn't the expression of faith. Maybe faith is just the reason we have hope. Maybe hope is the reason we have faith. Maybe it is a two-way street. I am not really sure it matters all that much. What matters is that we believe in something true, and we cherish every opportunity to testify to what is true so that the truth can be realized. Faith and hope allow us to do that. Faith and hope work together to give us fortitude and bring us blessing when we allow them to work through us. Think about it. Hope, by its very nature, lifts the soul and inspires thought... It opens the door to prayer. Have you ever looked at it that way? Have you ever thought of hope as being a resource for faith?

When we take the time to cherish and anticipate these truths, we instinctively open our hearts to its message. When you consider God as being that truth that, my friends, is what prayer is! That, in turn, feeds our faith... And our faith is thirsting for that nourishment. Our faith longs for that truth. It is in desperate need of that nourishment! So maybe when we hope, we should not look at it as a personal desire...even if that desire is based on truth. Maybe we should just look at it as a way to feed our faith. Maybe we should consider it validation for the soul only. All too often, I think we saddle hope with our own agendas and do not allow it to feed our faith as it should (I know I have). Maybe it has been the lack of that "nourishment" that has made our faith so weak?

Let's put this in terms of a simple analogy that everyone can relate to. We all know what happens to the human body when we eat a steady diet of junk food. We all know the importance of eating right and taking care of ourselves. Our spiritual health is no different. If we could put as much discipline and effort into taking care of our spiritual health (something we do not see) as we do our physical health (something we do see), can you imagine the results?

When we take care of our bodies, we start to feel better about ourselves. It motivates us to do even more. It drives us to maintain a level of excellence that allows us to be the best we can be on a consistent basis. When we filter our hopes through truth, we begin to feel better about our lives. It motivates us to do even more. It drives us to maintain a level of spirituality that allows us to be the best we can be on a consistent basis for others.

Of course, very few of us hang on to those diets. We all fall off the wagon from time to time. But we always seem to try and try again, and that is okay... We are only human after all. The fact that we think enough of ourselves to try is what matters. In the spiritual world, it is the same. My friend, forgiveness gets us right back on track every time. The point of all of this is the more we can nourish ourselves with the "good" stuff, the better off we will be. Our faith longs for the nourishment of God's truth. Hope allows us to contemplate that truth and open the door to its message. When we hope for "junk" instead of truth, well, that is usually what we get. Likewise, the more we can find true hope, the more nourishment we receive, and the more our faith is rewarded. Scripture lends credence to this as we read in Isaiah… "Those who hope in the Lord will renew their strength. They will soar on wings like eagles. They will run and not grow weary. They will walk and not be faint."

I want to share one more "Mom" story with you to help demonstrate this point of "nourished faith." Maybe when it is all said and done, you will understand why she was such an influence in my life. Let me just say, starting out, that it was not easy growing up with a saint (I say that affectionately, of course). The thing about my mother that you need to understand is everyone else came first, and if you lived with her, you pretty much had to adopt that same philosophy because there really was no argument against pure goodness. And when I say everyone, I mean every one! The little old neighborhood ladies, the church groups, the bridge club, sick relatives across town, and any other person who happened to stray into our yard. In addition to that, she was always quick to volunteer her children to help with these little "acts of love." I remember far too many occasions where I was pressed into action simply because I happened to be in the wrong place at the wrong time… Or was it the right place at the right time? That debate still rages on…

When I was growing up, it was commonplace to see people who were down on their luck, travel from town to town, looking for handouts. You can call them homeless, hobos, etc. I am not sure what the politically correct label is for these messengers of God's mercy. But when I was growing up, we called them tramps. My mother was quick to quiet this term from our mouths whenever one would show up, but I am sure it was heard a time or two in the way only the innocent honesty of children can get away with. Still we were often intrigued and felt only mildly intruded upon when they would show up at our doorstep. I am not sure my mother felt the same way, and I know my father was not always happy about the idea, but we just looked at it as something different that was happening for the day. As mentioned, we were often called into service to help deliver meals to these vagabonds who would sit in our yard, waiting for whatever Mom would happen to throw together for them... Many times, it was just a bowl of soup and a sandwich. They did not come around that often, but it happened with enough regularity that we were not taken aback by their arrival.

Over time, there was one "tramp" who became a regular at our house. We often speculated and wondered if he discovered Mom's great cooking and kept it a secret unto himself and somehow warded off the others so no other vagrants would come to visit because we stopped seeing anyone else but him. Many times, we would sit and talk to him as he ate, and I think he appreciated the interaction with us children... At least we thought so. He was always polite and always so very appreciative of everything Mom would do for him... every time! He was a walking work of mercy, and our mother was teaching us a valuable lesson about what it meant to feed the hungry and clothe the naked. My father tolerated it and understood, but even he, over time, began to wonder why he was such a "regular." We eventually learned he had a name, and he no longer became the tramp...even though that is how he is still referred to when we speak of him today.

My mother had little interaction with him. We would see him coming. We would run inside and yell, "Mom, the tramp is here!" He would sit in the shade of the apple tree. She would throw something together and put it on a tray. We would run it out to him, and he would finish and always leave us with the message "Be sure to tell your mom thank you" (which we did, most times). Sometimes, with the change of season, he would also ask us if we had any pieces of clothing that we could spare. Mom would see what we had and would always find a scarf or a pair of gloves lying around somewhere. In the winter, we would open the basement door so he could eat down there to get out of the cold while he ate. This went on for the better part of my childhood. I don't ever remember a time during my development when the tramp was not a part of my life.

One St. Patrick's Day, my father passed away. It was a very sad time for all of us, and my mother was especially affected, as you can imagine. My dad was admired by many, and I will never forget the outpouring of condolences my family received with his passing. Still it was a celebration of a life well lived, and even though he was not that old, there was an element of fulfillment that we all shared the day of his funeral. Perhaps the faith that he spent so much of his life sharing and writing about was now something we were experiencing together. On the day of the funeral, my entire family was gathered at the house after the ceremony. For anyone wondering, that was in excess of sixty people! During all of the reflection, camaraderie, and sharing, who should happen to show up at our doorstep but the tramp?

Not realizing what had happened, he came to our house and asked if we could spare a bite to eat. Some of my family members tried to explain to him that today was probably not a good day and explained to him the events of the day. He was saddened and extended his condolences. Other family members informed my mom that he had arrived and suggested that we turn him away. To many of us, this was not an unreasonable course of action. After all, we were not denying this man food, we were simply asking him to come at a more appropriate time. My mother simply said that would not be necessary. We had more than enough food there, and she fixed a plate for him. I dare say he ate better that day than he had ever eaten before.

My mother showed the depth of her faith to my entire family that day...and it gets better. Once the tramp was done eating, he wondered if we might have anything to keep him warm as the nights were still pretty chilly. My mother went to her closet and pulled out a relatively new jacket that my father had been wearing and gave it to us to give to him. This was her husband of forty-plus years who she had just buried that day, and she was giving a piece of his clothing away that he had just worn four days prior to someone in need. The smell of Dad had not even left the garment, and she did not hesitate. Some of us were taken aback by the gesture. Some even quipped how Dad was so wary of this man, and now here he was with his jacket. Some were unnerved that this man would have the gall to ask, knowing the events of the day. Most of us, however…all of us…were in complete awe of my mother.

I am sure you have all read stories or have seen the movies where the lowly are really angels in disguise and other people's kindness is rewarded. This one could not have been scripted any better…and we did not get to read it in a book or see it in a movie…we got to live it. To make this script even better, I will mention that I do not recall the tramp coming back to our house after that day. If he did, it was not for too many more times. We never knew what happened to him. He just stopped coming. I will let you figure it out.

And that is what I call "nourished faith." When we exercise our faith and feed it through hope, we are strengthening our spirit. When we have faith in something true, and we cherish our opportunities to act based on that truth, then good things happen. Our virtues are not something to aspire to, they are meant to inspire. Faith and hope are more than a way to think and feel. They are a way to live.

- Cherish opportunities to testify to what is true so truth can be realized.
- Hope lifts the spirit and inspires thought… It opens the door to prayer.
- Nourished faith is fed with hope.
- Virtues are not something to aspire to, they are meant to inspire.
- Exercise your faith…strengthen your spirit.

CHAPTER 10

O Ye of Little Faith

I have a question for you scholars out there. Did hope and faith exist while Jesus walked the earth? Why? Why was there a need for them? Allow me to qualify that question. Do you think the followers of Jesus had hope and faith while Jesus was alive? If so, what more could they have hoped for? What more could they have believed in? I suppose the answer to that question is yes. Anyone still on earth would probably need some semblance of those virtues... Even Jesus Himself perhaps? Still I do not recall any excerpts from the Bible where Jesus claimed to need faith. He was God's Son after all! I recall nothing of Him hoping for anything He did not already possess! Even in His darkest moments, when He asked that this cup pass from Him, He did not express hope or have faith that it would happen. He only expressed obedience...obedience to the end. When He raised Lazarus from the dead, He did not express hope or faith that it would happen, only thanksgiving for being heard.

I would speculate, however, that His followers still needed hope and faith, since they did not fully realize who Christ was. In fact, their hopes were probably quite high, even though their faith was still very weak. "You believe because you have seen me. Blessed are those who have not seen but still believe."

The point of the question is, when you have it all, what else is there to need? The disciples realized, albeit too late, perhaps what they had in Jesus. It is very easy to believe in something when you can see it and get to know it firsthand. In fact, when you possess that knowledge, it is fair to say that faith is no longer needed. The very definition of faith is trusting in something that is not tangible. It is only when that which was tangible is taken from us that we begin to have faith again. In the case of the disciples, they did not need to have faith in Jesus, per se. They knew Him. They broke bread with Him and lived with Him. Instead their faith centered on the message of His word and His resurrection, and they used their own inspired words to spread that message and recount the events of His life. It is through the Word that we have all come to know Jesus and have come to believe in Him. This, in and of itself, can be considered a miracle. Think about it. If you take this at face value, what I am saying is our faith is based on the message of the written word that has been handed down through generations. Our faith has been built on two thousand years of hearsay! If not for the grace of God and the power of the Holy Spirit, this word should never have survived.

I don't care how good the story might have been... It should not have survived. But it did survive, and not only survive, but grew and thrived and multiplied and spread across the entire planet...and it is still growing! How is that not a miracle? I can assure you no human effort alone could have made that happen... We are not that good. Working through us, however, God's Word has lived on. We have been an instrument of His miracle. How cool is that? Before we nominate ourselves for sainthood, we should acknowledge that some of us have played a bigger role in this miracle than others. But any time we have taken the time to testify to the truth, we have allowed this faith to breathe and have life. Likewise, any time we have doubted this truth and stood in the way of its expansion, we have stifled its growth. And let's face it, there is a doubting Thomas in all of us.

"Your faith has healed you." How many times do we hear that phrase in our readings at church and read it in the Bible? Jesus says this over and over again, prior to making the blind see and the lame walk. What an empowering statement to make! In essence, what Jesus is saying is we have control of our own well-being...as long as we believe in Him. In other words, with God, all things are possible.

All we have to do is believe it! Still, for some reason, we are fearful of that power. We don't believe it is possible, and we do not trust ourselves with it… "O ye of little faith."

I have often wondered how those people Jesus cured felt after their encounter with Him and hearing those words? What did He mean by "My faith has healed me"? Maybe they were too ecstatic about being cured that they didn't give it too much thought. Or maybe they knew exactly what he meant and didn't think to question it. If so, why didn't they share it and why didn't we hear about it? When Jesus said, "If you have faith the size of a mustard seed, you can say to this mulberry tree, 'Be uprooted and transplanted in the sea.' And it would obey you." Wouldn't you think someone in the crowd might have said, "Yeah, right"? Or don't you think someone would have tried to make that happen? How many trees were uprooted that day, I wonder? Where is that documented? Still this is the power we possess when we believe. But alas, our faith is so weak we can't even fill a mustard seed.

Because of this, we continually doubt ourselves and our God. We let reality dictate on a daily basis how our day is going to go, and there is seemingly nothing we can do about it. We are so quick to give up hope and lose faith because…well, today just wasn't our day. Maybe tomorrow will be better…or next week. Have you ever noticed how when we get sad, we have a tendency to give up on things? Things that we used to feel were important just don't feel that way anymore. Or we just don't care?

The same relationship exists with hope and faith. When we give up hope, we stop believing. One could speculate that it is the absence of hope that causes our sadness. When we have nothing to look forward to, when we have nothing to cherish with anticipation, then we are inviting sadness into our lives. I don't need to tell you how much sadness life can dish out. I also don't need to tell you how much joy life can bring to us when we know where to look. Therefore the key to it all and perhaps the key to this whole "nutshell" is knowing where to look. This is why I believe finding the truth in what we hope for is so important. When our focus is on the truth, we begin to filter things more clearly, and we are more in control of our own reality.

The thing that has truly boggled my mind is that with all of this reflection, all of the centuries of theology and religious example, we are still looking at less than a mustard seed. You would think that with all of the technological advances and know-how we have accumulated, been blessed with, and privy to, the one thing we would have learned to appreciate more and more is the unknown. Instead we continue to only put our faith in what is and still fear what we do not understand. The good news, if you want to call it good news, is we are not alone. We have been doing this from the beginning… So why break tradition? Why indeed?

Scripture is filled with one account after another of man's feeble attempts at faith, starting with Adam all the way through Peter's denial of Jesus and beyond…all through history…even up to a minute ago when I was praying for an answer to a problem. Recall the time when Jesus walked out to the disciples on the stormy sea, and Peter asked to join Him. He got out of the boat but began to sink and cried out, "My Lord, help me" (my exact words a minute ago, by the way)! Jesus was right there! He had his back, and Peter had nothing to worry about, but he still could not believe…because it was just too unbelievable, I guess. Time after time after time, we fall flat on our face and still Jesus can say to us, "Your faith has healed you."

God has to be smiling at us. I am certain of it. We must be a source of great entertainment for our heavenly Father. Probably not unlike the entertainment we get raising our own children. Maybe God is trying to teach us how to ride a spiritual bike. That is the only thing I can liken it to. He knows we can do it. He encourages our efforts. He is just waiting for us to believe it too.

Let's go with that scenario for a minute… When we were learning to ride a bike, we had to know what the pedals did, what the handlebars were for, how we made it go and stop…all well and good. Assuming we had all of that down there was still no guarantee we were going to be able to take off on that thing and be good at it. Many of us had the skinned knees, bruised elbows, and possible stitches to prove it! The only thing that ultimately allowed us to conquer the art of riding a bike was balance. No one could show us where that was.

No one could show us how it worked or how to make it start and stop… It was all on us…or should I say in us.

Faith is balance. How is that for turning a phrase? When we look for the definition of faith, it is often defined as "believing in God or the doctrines of a religion being based on spiritual apprehension rather than proof." Can anyone "prove" balance (just curious)? Is faith really believing in something that isn't there? Or is it believing in something that is…just not seen? And even more importantly, is it believing in something that is…just not seen…but felt? Just like balance, why shouldn't it be real and why shouldn't it be felt?

I have a little bit of a complaint to lodge with my Catholic religion. I don't know who wrote the prayer. I don't know if a council of bishops got together and thought this up or if someone just jotted it down and everyone thought it was a good idea. But many times, when I have attended baptisms or have attended services where we renew our baptismal promises, we go through the creed. The priest asks us to confirm our belief in God, in Jesus, and the Holy Spirit to which we all respond with a resounding "I DO." At the end, the priest summarizes by saying, "This is our faith." Invariably, I cringe…no it's not! This is not our faith! This is just what we believe. These are the tools through which our faith is expressed. These are the pedals, the handlebars, and the tires that make it all happen. Our faith is the balance. Our faith is not a proclamation. It is a feeling…a sensation, if you will.

I spoke earlier of our team approach to CCD classes. Another exercise we liked to do and one I took with me to my later classes outside of the team setting was the Bible story about Jesus's encounter with the blind man on the road to Jericho. The story from Luke goes like this:

> Jesus approached Jericho. A blind man was sitting by the roadside, begging. When he heard the crowd going by, he asked what was happening. They told him, "Jesus of Nazareth is passing by."

85

He called out, "Jesus, Son of David, have mercy on me!"

Those who led the way rebuked him and told him to be quiet, but he shouted all the more, "Son of David, have mercy on me!"

Jesus stopped and ordered the man to be brought to him. When he came near, Jesus asked him, "What do you want me to do for you?"

"Lord, I want to see," he replied.

Jesus said to him, "Receive your sight. Your faith has healed you." Immediately he received his sight and followed Jesus, praising God. When all the people saw it, they also praised God.

Throughout this exercise, we had the students close their eyes. We asked them to put themselves in the blind man's shoes and pretend that they could no longer see. We tried to recreate for them the environment this man had to deal with in that everyone was telling him to be quiet and not treating him with any respect. We stressed the importance of the blind man's words "Lord, I want to see." While this passage was being read, we would quietly darken the room so that by the time the reading was done and the students opened their eyes, all they could see was a single light in the middle of the room…a light which symbolized the light of Christ. It was borderline dramatic but when taken with the right degree of reflection, it sent a very powerful message about what it meant to have hope and faith…and to see.

I tell this story to prove my point. The blind man knew nothing of the Nicene Creed. He did not know of the Holy Spirit or the Trinity or the resurrection of the dead, the Communion of saints, the forgiveness of sins, or even life everlasting. All he knew was that he wanted to see…and he wanted Jesus to have mercy on him. That's it! He wanted it so badly he could not be silenced. It is as if he knew that his whole life depended on it. His whole being "felt" it… And Jesus said to him, "Your faith has healed you." I don't know about you, but I must have prayed the creed over a thousand times, but I don't ever remember being that passionate about it. I don't ever remember feeling my faith the way this blind man did.

- Testify to the truth. Be a part of the miracle.
- With God, all things are possible… Believe it.
- Don't let reality dictate who you will be today… Find joy.
- Faith is like balance. It is real and it is felt. Find your inner peace.

CHAPTER 11

Faith Can Move Mountains

And maybe it all comes down to that…feeling our faith. It poses the question then, has our faith gotten stronger or weaker over the years? Maybe that is a question for the individual and not for the masses. But in so much as we are all one body, it is fair to say one will affect the other. My father used to write about a "faith crisis." He likened it to the energy crisis of the early '70s. He spoke of how we were humanizing God and exalting humanity. Being influenced by the '70s, I remember thinking, *He just didn't get it.* Deep down, however, I also remember fearing he might be right and hoping he was just filtering things a little too sternly. Ironically I am now at the age he was when he wrote about that subject, and I still have the same perceptions…and the same fears. The following is an example of my dad's writing, which lends itself to the point I am trying to make:

> I see God's will through the eyes of faith. I do His will through love. Faith inspires my thoughts, and love inspires my actions. In spite of all knowledge and human accomplishment, this is still God's world. He created it. My sole purpose of existence is to do His will. Unless I am prepared to completely rebel against God, I am going to do His will willingly (which is the way to inner peace) or unwillingly (which is the way

to inner conflict). The choice is mine. The choice is not easy in the world I see around me. It means there is no time for the inner life. (EJS)

The faith crisis may be real, but to my way of thinking, it has been in crisis mode from the beginning. Why is it so hard for us to get over the hump of the mustard seed? If humanizing God is going to help us to relate to Him better, isn't that a good thing? So long as we do not manipulate His teaching to fit our own reality? Isn't celebrating our human accomplishments and bettering our fellow man a wonderful thing? So long as we do not deem ourselves equal to God or deny His significance in our lives? I realize that is walking a very thin line, and we are exposing ourselves to those pitfalls, but it is still possible.

Still my father makes an excellent point with regard to inner peace and inner conflict. God's will, shall be done…willingly or unwillingly…or even unknowingly. Finding that balance and understanding…no, "feeling" that connection between bounty and blessing, between found and unknown, between reality and truth is what will bring us inner peace and allow our faith to heal us.

It could very well be that this is the reason our faith is weak. Just as hope becomes generic in meaning and loses its true value to us, perhaps faith is also diluted by our feeble attempts to label it and lay claim to it. Faith is not a building or a blueprint for a car that can be improved upon and revamped (nor does it need to be), it is a feeling (and not everyone has it). Because it is a feeling, it is a very personal thing for us. Even though it is shared by a lot of us, it is still personal.

Feelings cannot be taught, only experienced. Because of this, each generation must experience for themselves what prior generations already have (or hope to have). Thank God for this! What this means then is that even though there may be a lot of reinventing of the wheel going on, with each life, there is the promise of a renewal of faith, a rebirth of God's message. What a glorious way to keep things fresh, inspired, and perpetuated! As we have plainly demonstrated, if faith were left up to us, we would fail miserably. Faith is a gift from God, and it is freely given to whomever He reveals it to…and His will shall be done. The best we can do is to share our experiences and "hope" the truth will live on. That is our single most basic calling as Christians…to testify to the truth. For this reason, I would dare to respectfully disagree with my father. Faith is not in crisis, education is. Faith is not ours to pass on…truth is. Opening our hearts to truth will open our souls to faith, if God so wills it.

Just like all the other things we know to be true, we must first learn what we can about it. But in the end, it is what we experience and how we apply that knowledge that makes us proficient at what we do…and grow from it. This is how basically all of our discoveries and accomplishments are achieved. There is something to be said for this. These things have so much to do with the quality of life that we enjoy…but they have little to do with life itself…just ask the tramp. This is the misnomer that repeats itself with every generation. While we bask in the glow of our accomplishments, we must realize and never forget our accomplishments mean very little if we do not do them for others. Man has made some truly wonderful things! But it is still God's world. It is the feeling of balance, the sensation we get from living together that defines life for us. That is the life God created and always wanted for us. That is the truth we must testify to… along with God's love and presence in this world.

"Faith can move mountains." How many mountains do we have in our lives that need moved? How many obstacles? How many of these obstacles are causing us the inner conflict my dad spoke of earlier? I know all too well how difficult it is to come face-to-face with this inner conflict. But it isn't until we confront these obstacles that we can come to terms with some of the mistakes we have been making. It is a very bitter pill to swallow, and if not taken with a lot of hope and faith, it could very easily do us in.

Earlier I mentioned that when we forgive, we give hope. When we are forgiven, we receive hope. Imagine the joy of being able to forgive ourselves. Recognizing and dealing with these obstacles is one of the best ways we have to open ourselves to the truth and nourish our faith. If you think about it, maybe these are the mulberry trees Jesus was talking about. Laying down our burdens and letting them go is not unlike uprooting a tree, is it not? Believe it.

I don't know about you, but I often catch myself thinking that I am the only one with problems in the world…or at least thinking no one has more problems than I do. I am always worrying about this or that and always wondering why things never seem to work in my favor. Sometimes I even feel like it is deliberate, like I am cursed or something. I feel like a modern-day Job. The book of Job, now there is a guy I can relate to. I would have to say it is my favorite Old Testament book. I like it because it is reality TV at its finest. We have a candid dialogue between Job and God. Job has no qualms with letting God know how he feels and expressing his frustrations… I do that pretty much daily.

Job is hit with one unfortunate occurrence after another, and his day is filled with just trying to maintain and keep a cool head about things (sound familiar?). His world is falling apart, and his friends are trying to tell him what to do, yet he sticks with the plan because it is the right thing to do. He does not take his frustrations out on others, and he doesn't place blame. He is very much like the blind man on the road to Jericho… He just wants to understand (see), and he wants God to have mercy. That may very well encapsulate about 90 percent of my recent prayer life. Who doesn't feel as Job did? Who hasn't prayed for these things themselves at some point in their lives? In the end, God makes amends with Job. He rewards Job for his faith, patience, perseverance, and undying hope despite all odds. Job moved mountains because he had faith. He held on…not because he figured he would be rewarded eventually…not because he enjoyed the sympathy he was getting from his friends. He held on simply because it was the right thing to do. He testified to the truth.

When we do the right thing in the light of what is true, then our tough decisions get a little easier. Our solutions may not always be easier, but our decisions are. A popular catchphrase of my youth to get people thinking this way was "What would Jesus do?" We would see it on bumper stickers and use it in classrooms, all in the attempt to get us doing the right thing. I always thought this was a nice slogan, but I always felt too much pressure from it. Who am I to know what Jesus would do? This almost sounds like an essay question for a religion test. Did I miss an assignment somewhere? Was there a cheat sheet somewhere that I could borrow that would have all the right answers? Still I would like to resurrect this slogan. I think it's time has come again…but I would change it up this time. I would personalize it. "Forget what Jesus would do. What would *you* do if you were going to do the right thing?" The answers may vary and make for some interesting results but at least it would hopefully get us to take a look at that question honestly and find the answer from within.

And that is the point. Faith (like hope) is found within. God is the giver of faith, and when we have been deemed recipients of it, it is ours to cherish and administer. Faith is not a commodity. It cannot be purchased (it is already paid for). It cannot be obtained from an outside source…and it is NOT inherited. Not even the Eucharist can give us faith. The sacraments are not a guarantee of faith. They are only a way to prepare ourselves to become worthy of the gift and a means to nourish that faith once it is received. When we are given faith, God sees in us a venue for His Word to be spread despite all odds, and it becomes our responsibility to care for that message… Our inner peace depends on it. Our reluctance to do this only creates obstacles for ourselves. We are being asked to uproot trees and clear a path so our collective hopes will be fulfilled. We have the power to do that because we were given faith! All we have to do is believe it.

Faith then is as strong as we are… Faith is as strong as you are. Are you feeling up to the challenge? We are being asked to testify to the truth, plain and simple. We are being asked to do the right thing. When we learn to embrace that calling and anticipate opportunities to put that faith to work, we are spreading hope. We are planting seed on fertile soil… We begin to see the fruits of our labors, hope grows, and faith is nourished… We become part of the miracle.

- Faith cannot be taught, only experienced.
- What would you do if you were going to do the right thing?
- Opening your heart to truth will open your soul to faith.
- Lay down your burdens… Uproot your trees… Your faith has healed you.
- Let your virtues flow from within… Move mountains.
- Testify to the truth… Pass it on.

CHAPTER 12

The Greatest of These Is Love

Though faith, as a gift from God, may be a little harder to come by, love is freely given, and it is everywhere! The relationship between faith, hope, and love is very intriguing to contemplate. Love allows us to think ideally and reach beyond ourselves. In many ways, hope does the same thing. Hope allows us to believe in things that love tells our hearts is true… We feel it. The more we experience love, the more hope we find. The deeper our love evolves, the stronger our hopes become. When our love transcends reality…when our love becomes unconditional, our hopes become sanctified. When God reveals the depth of His love for us, through that hope, faith is given, and we are forever changed.

Hope may start in the darkness, but it is the light of love that allows hope to shine. Jesus comes to bring hope to the sinner, but what He is really bringing us is God's love. Hope is a way for us to feel love when nothing else can. That is how precious hope is…and how powerful love is! Love reaches the darkest corners of our lives to bring a message of hope. When we walk in the light of that hope, we begin to see promise, we begin to cherish and anticipate, we begin to believe.

In the earlier chapters, I explored the subject of love as it pertained to relationships. I was careful not to emphasize God too much as I wanted to focus on the gift we are to each other and the discoveries that can be made when we seek love together. It was my hope that in doing so, couples might come to the realization on their own that once they reach that level of intimacy and mutual individuality by sharing their core values in a spirit of forgiveness, they would, in fact, be finding God.

That is the beauty of it all! That is the power we possess. We have the ability to bring God's hope and love to each other through reconciliation and forgiveness…and not only as couples but as individuals. Love truly is an amazing thing! Human history has been defined by it. We have come to emphasize love as something very real in our lives. We know it exists because we have felt it in our hearts. We recognize love as a truth because we have experienced it firsthand and have seen what it can do. Earlier I made the claim that hope and faith are founded in truth. And they are! Anyone who acknowledges the presence of love as a truth must also acknowledge the presence of hope and faith as a part of that same truth.

Love is so prevalent that we do not even think to question it. What would happen if we viewed hope and faith with the same degree of confidence? Conversely we have spent a lot of time talking about the power we could possess if we would only believe. If our hope and faith is lifted to the point where we are inspired to action, and our faith is still only the size of a mustard seed, how much greater can it get? If we can love each other this much in an imperfect world, how much greater then can we love and be loved in a perfect world? Just like when Peter stepped onto the water, it would be too unbelievable to be believable… Welcome to heaven.

Faith, hope, and love are tied together and forever joined. Not unlike the Son, the Spirit, and the Father themselves, the virtues are very much like the Trinity. The faith of the Son, the Spirit of hope, and the love of the Father are all working together to inspire our hearts and bring meaning to our existence. So when life gives us mountains, we now know what to do with them. When our lives stand at a crossroads, we know which path to take because we have love in our hearts, faith to guide us, and hope to inspire us. And just as these virtues are expressed from within us, so too is the Trinity.

With so much power, how can our faith be weak? How can our hopes be in vain? How can our love be hidden?

For when we die…
We will have no need of Hope, for our hopes will be fulfilled.
We will have no need of Faith, for we will possess what we believe.
But we shall always love… Love lives eternal. (EJS)

FINDING HOPE

Amid the trials of reflection,
Between the heartache of what was
And the remorse of what should have been,
There lies an ember of a youth remembered.
Within that ember lies a seed.
Not of dreams or forgotten passions,
But of a spirit that has stood the test of time.
Within that spirit there is light.
A light that gives meaning to our heartache,
And a purpose to which all things must give answer.
Within that purpose there is truth.
A truth through which all things are made new,
Every day a new beginning...
And each hope, founded in truth, a reality.

(CS [EC] '18)

ABOUT THE AUTHOR

E ugene Christopher (aka Christopher E. Shonk) is new to the lit-
erary scene but very much enjoys the power of the written word.
Chris grew up in a large family from southeast Ohio, where he still
resides. Many of Chris's childhood memories and adult experiences
are shared in this book. Chris uses these experiences to give us a fresh
and intriguing perspective on his search for truth and meaning in his
life and, in so doing, challenges us to do the same.

CPSIA information can be obtained
at www.ICGtesting.com
Printed in the USA
JSHW040159170423
40341JS00006B/163